· A ·
GOOD·BOOK
· IS THE ·
PRECIOUS
LIFE-BLOOD
· OF A ·
MASTER
SPIRIT
Milton

PRINTED IN GREAT BRITAIN

The KINGS TREASURIES
OF LITERATURE

GENERAL EDITOR
SIR A·T· QUILLER COUCH

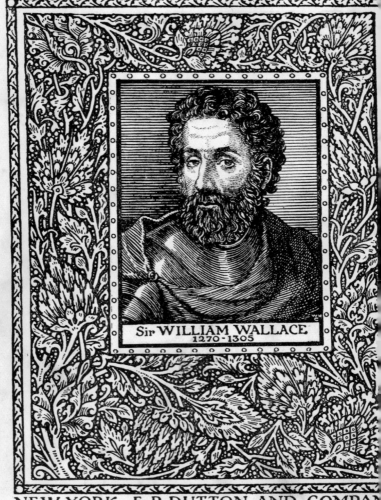

Sir WILLIAM WALLACE
1270 - 1305

NEW YORK   E·P·DUTTON AND COMPAN

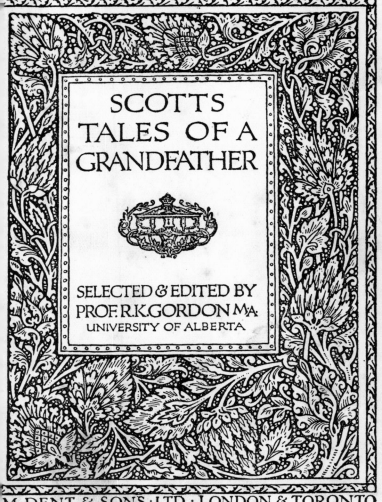

SCOTTS TALES OF A GRANDFATHER

SELECTED & EDITED BY
PROF. R.K.GORDON M.A.
UNIVERSITY OF ALBERTA

J.M·DENT & SONS ·LTD · LONDON & TORONTO

First Published in this Edition   .   1925
Reprinted 1928, 1929

PRINTED IN GREAT BRITAIN

CONTENTS

INTRODUCTION

THE best part of Scott's life and the best of his books belong to the Scottish Border country. Though he was born in Edinburgh (15th August, 1771), his family had been Borderers for generations. His father was the first to desert the green hills by the Tweed for a town life. Scott was true to the blood of his ancestors, and his happiest years were spent on the Borders. There he found many of the stories and the persons out of which he made his books, there he bought land and built his great house of Abbotsford, and when he felt his death draw near he was not content to lay his bones far away from Tweed.

Scott came of fighting stock. His forbears had long been known and feared in the old riding and raiding days of wars between England and Scotland, when men followed

> The simple plan
> That they should take who have the power
> And they should keep who can.

Though Scott was the son of a cautious and devout Edinburgh lawyer, he inherited the courage and daring of his rough and ready forefathers. But he was born in peaceful days and had to be content with describing in books the exploits which, if he had lived in earlier times, he would have performed. His stories in verse and in prose owe much of their life and fire to the hot Border blood which came to him from his freebooting ancestors. He himself would have been a soldier but for physical unfitness.

7

This disability was the result of a fever when he was
eighteen months old which left his right foot helpless.
He was sent for a change to his grandfather's farmhouse,
Sandy Knowe, on the banks of the Tweed. Here various
remedies were tried for his lameness. Whenever a sheep
was killed for the use of the family the child was stripped
and wrapped in the warm fleece. But Scott never got rid
of his trouble altogether. He grew to be a very strong
man, but limped to the end of his life. It shows how
real Scott's ancestors were to his imagination that he
was comforted by finding that two of his forefathers
had suffered from the same deformity.

This visit to Sandy Knowe was never forgotten. It was
his first sight of the Borders. He was often carried out
to the fields by the cow-bailie to spend all day among the
flocks. Once he was forgotten and was only remembered
after a thunderstorm had come on. He was found lying
on his back clapping his hands at the lightning and crying
out, "Bonny! bonny!" at every flash. At Sandy Knowe
his grandmother told him many old tales of Border
heroes whose deeds were still remembered in the countryside. He would also act the battles of the Scots and the
English with shells and pebbles ranged on the floor.
In this way, and not as a task, Scott began to learn
history. Reading soon followed. "I cannot at this
moment," he wrote fifty years later, "tell how or when
I learned to read, but it was by fits and snatches, as
one aunt or another in the old rumble-tumble farmhouses
could give me a lesson, and I am sure it increased my
love and habit of reading more than the austerities of
a school could have done."

The happy open-air life at Sandy Knowe improved the
lad's health. When strong and big enough to ride on a
small Shetland pony instead of the cow-bailie's shoulder,

he was recalled to his father's rather gloomy house in
George's Square, Edinburgh. Soon afterwards, in his
eighth year, he entered the High School. Here he was
soon popular, and no wonder. Nobody else in the school
could tell such stories, and he entered eagerly into all
sports where his lameness did not prevent him. As he
could not fight standing up he met his opponents sitting
tied to a board. Before he left school he could climb
the "kittle nine steps," a pass on the brink of the Castle
rock so narrow that only a goat or a High School boy
could turn the corner of the building without falling
over the precipice. In other adventures outside of school
he was also a ringleader. One of these, that in which
Green-breeks figured, he remembered to the end of
his life.

The tale must be told in his own words. "It is well
known that there is little boxing at the Scottish schools.
About forty or fifty years ago, however, a far more
dangerous mode of fighting, in parties or factions, was
permitted in the streets of Edinburgh, to the great disgrace of the police, and danger of the parties concerned.
These parties were generally formed from the quarters
of the town in which the combatants resided, those of a
particular square or district fighting against those of an
adjoining one. Hence it happened that the children of
the higher classes were often pitted against those of the
lower, each taking their side according to the residence
of their friends. So far as I recollect, however, it was
unmingled either with feelings of democracy or aristo-
cracy, or indeed with malice or ill-will of any kind towards
the opposite party. In fact, it was only a rough mode of
play. Such contests were, however, maintained with
great vigour with stones, and sticks, and fisticuffs, when
one party dared to charge, and the other stood their
*

ground. Of course, mischief sometimes happened; boys are said to have been killed at these *bickers*, as they were called, and serious accidents certainly took place, as many contemporaries can bear witness.

"The author's father residing in George's Square, in the southern side of Edinburgh, the boys belonging to that family, with others in the square, were arranged into a sort of company, to which a lady of distinction presented a handsome set of colours. Now, this company or regiment, as a matter of course, was engaged in weekly warfare with the boys inhabiting the Cross-Causeway, Bristo Street, the Potter Row—in short, the neighbouring suburbs. These last were chiefly of the lower rank, but hardy loons, who threw stones to a hair's-breadth, and were very rugged antagonists at close quarters. The skirmish sometimes lasted for a whole evening, until one party or the other was victorious, when, if ours were successful, we drove the enemy to their quarters, and were usually chased back by the reinforcement of bigger lads who came to their assistance. If, on the contrary, we were pursued, as was often the case, into the precincts of our square, we were in our turn supported by our elder brothers, domestic servants, and similar auxiliaries. It followed, from our frequent opposition to each other, that, though not knowing the names of our enemies, we were yet well acquainted with their appearance, and had nicknames for the most remarkable of them. One very active and spirited boy might be considered as the principal leader in the cohort of the suburbs. He was, I suppose, thirteen or fourteen years old, finely made, tall, blue-eyed, with long fair hair, the very picture of a youthful Goth. This lad was always first in the charge, and last in the retreat—the Achilles at once and Ajax of the Cross-Causeway. He was too formidable to us not

to have a cognomen, and, like that of a knight of old,
it was taken from the most remarkable part of his dress,
being a pair of old green livery breeches, which was the
principal part of his clothing; for, like Pentapolin,
according to Don Quixote's account, Green-breeks, as
we called him, always entered the battle with bare arms,
legs, and feet.

"It fell, that once upon a time when the combat was
at its thickest, this plebeian champion headed a charge
so rapid and furious, that all fled before him. He was
several paces before his comrades, and had actually laid
his hands upon the patrician standard, when one of
our party, whom some misjudging friend had entrusted
with a *couteau de chasse*, or hanger, inspired with a zeal
for the honour of the corps, worthy of Major Sturgeon
himself, struck poor Green-breeks over the head, with
sufficient strength to cut him down. When this was
seen, the casualty was so far beyond what had ever
taken place before, that both parties fled different ways,
leaving poor Green-breeks, with his bright hair plentifully dabbled in blood, to the care of the watchman, who
(honest man) took care not to know who had done the
mischief. The bloody hanger was thrown into one of the
Meadow ditches, and solemn secrecy was sworn on all
hands; but the remorse and terror of the actor were
beyond all bounds, and his apprehensions of the most
dreadful character. The wounded hero was for a few
days in the Infirmary, the case being only a trifling one.
But though inquiry was strongly pressed on him, no
argument could make him indicate the person from whom
he had received the wound, though he must have been
perfectly well known to him. When he recovered and
was dismissed, the author and his brothers opened a communication with him, through the medium of a popular

gingerbread baker, of whom both parties were customers, in order to tender a subsidy in the name of smart-money. The sum would excite ridicule were I to name it; but sure I am that the pockets of the noted Green-breeks never held as much money of his own. He declined the remittance, saying that he would not sell his blood; but at the same time reprobated the idea of being an informer, which he said was *clam,* that is, base or mean. With much urgency, he accepted a pound of snuff for the use of some old woman—aunt, grandmother, or the like—with whom he lived. We did not become friends, for the *bickers* were more agreeable to both parties than any more pacific amusement; but we conducted them ever after under mutual assurances of the highest consideration for each other."

In the class-room Scott was less prominent, and was generally in the middle of the form, though a brilliant answer sometimes sent him to the top. He was fond of telling of one of his successes. "There was a boy in my class at school," he said, "who stood always at the top, nor could I with all my efforts supplant him. Day came after day, and still he kept his place, do what I would; till at length I observed that, when a question was asked him, he always fumbled at a particular button in the lower part of his waistcoat. To remove it, therefore, became expedient in my eyes; and in an evil moment it was removed with a knife. Great was my anxiety to know the success of my measure; and it succeeded too well. When the boy was again questioned, his fingers sought again for the button, but it was not to be found. In his distress he looked down for it; it was to be seen no more than to be felt. He stood confounded, and I took possession of his place; nor did he ever recover it, or ever, I believe, suspect who was the author of his wrong." Scott's most eager reading was of history, stories of adventure and romance, fairy tales, and odd volumes of Shakespeare.

At Edinburgh University, where he began to take classes in 1783, he continued to satisfy his own appetite in reading and to neglect the ordinary work of the classroom. His great delight was to escape on Saturdays and during the vacations to a sheltered rocky nook high up on Arthur's Seat, Salisbury Crags, or Blackford Hill, and there with his friend, John Irving, to read and invent endless tales of romantic adventure. An illness about this time gave him still larger opportunities for losing himself in the wonderland of books. All this pleasant, idle, unsystematic reading was, though Scott did not know it, part of his training to be one of the great story-tellers of the world.

It was his father's desire that Walter should follow the law, and on the boy's recovery he took his seat in the office. The drudgery was irksome, though he could work as hard as anyone on occasion and once wrote 120 pages without food or rest. The pocket money earned by such tasks was spent on theatres and books. Occasional expeditions to the Highlands, sometimes on legal business, were a welcome change, and introduced him to scenes and people which he recalled long afterwards when he came to write his novels. Anything which roused Scott's interest seemed to be held for ever by his wonderful memory. Among the Highlanders he met was Alexander Stewart of Invernahyle who told the eager boy stories of his experiences in the insurrections of 1715 and 1745. There were also excursions on foot or horseback to places of historical interest nearer home. Scott also belonged to literary societies and had his full share in all the pranks and amusements of Edinburgh law-students.

Few of his friends knew that these years saw the

beginning and end of the only deep love affair of Scott's life. His suit was not successful, but he kept his suffering to himself. It was not his way to complain much of misfortunes, but he confessed about thirty years later that the crack would remain in his heart till his dying day. About 1790 he settled down to hard legal study. Every morning he walked two miles to the house of his friend, William Clerk, and got him out of bed to his task before seven o'clock. In 1792 he was called to the Bar to the great satisfaction of his father, who would have been little pleased to know that his son would be remembered as a poet and novelist and not as a lawyer or a judge.

Scott's heart was never in his profession, though he practised it for several years. Gradually other tastes and desires drew him into other paths, though it was some time before he decided to accept authorship as a career. Like most great writers he drifted into literature. In the vacations he left law behind him and was away to the Borders or the Highlands. With Robert Shortreed he penetrated the wildest districts of the Borders, making friends in every house, picking up curious old relics such as war-horns, and collecting ballads which had been handed down by word of mouth among the descendants of the moss-troopers. All this was valuable later, for Scott was an author who lived and learned much in the open air. "He was makin' himsel' a' the time," as Shortreed said, "but he didna ken maybe what he was about till years had passed; at first he thought o' little, I dare say, but the queerness and the fun."

When he was kept in Edinburgh he took keen pleasure in acting as quartermaster in the Edinburgh Light Horse, a body of volunteer cavalry, organised for fear of French invasion. Scott was always passionately fond of riding, and declared that a regiment of horse had been exercising through his head since he was five years old. When he was educating his boys and girls he put love of horsemanship next to love of truth, and taught his children his own fearlessness.

At the end of 1797 Scott married Miss Carpenter, and in the following summer removed to Lasswade Cottage on the Esk, about six miles from Edinburgh. Here were spent some of the happiest moments of his life. He had friends in the neighbourhood, and he was beginning to find out that he was a poet.

> Sweet are the paths, O passing sweet,
> By Esk's fair streams that run,
> O'er airy steep, thro' copsewood deep
> Impervious to the sun.

In 1799 he was appointed Sheriff of Selkirk, a post which secured him £300 a year without taking up too much of his time. His duties necessitated delightful expeditions through his beloved Border country and gave him further chances of collecting old ballads. These he finally decided to publish, and the necessary work formed his chief amusement during the winters in Edinburgh and the summers at Lasswade. The ballad collection appeared in 1802 and 1803 under the title of *The Minstrelsy of the Scottish Border*. Its success brought fame, but did not at once decide him to make literature the chief business of his life. He had, however, given up hopes of rising in law and began to see that he could make his fortune through the booksellers.

In May 1804 Scott changed his summer quarters to Ashestiel on the banks of the Tweed in order to conform to the regulations which required the Sheriff of Selkirk to reside part of the year in the district. Here among the hills in a little farm-house with an old-fashioned garden Scott passed eight or nine summers, probably the happiest in his life. He had sufficient wealth from his poetry and other writings, but was not yet bothered by droves of tourists coming to stare at the famous author. Nor was he yet distracted by land-buying and by building. His health was excellent, and his young family was growing up around him. "Here we live all the summer like little kings," he wrote to one of his friends, "and only wish that you could take a scamper with me over the hills in the morning, and return to a clean tablecloth, a leg of forest mutton, and a blazing hearth in the afternoon." Scott's day began at five o'clock; by six he was at his desk with his papers and books about him and with a favourite dog near at hand watching his master. By breakfast time he had "broken the neck of the day's work." Another spell of writing followed breakfast, and at noon he was free to walk, ride, fish, or hunt. Few men have written so much as Scott; fewer still have found time for so many other interests.

The winters were passed in Edinburgh, for

> When silvan occupation's done,
> And o'er the chimney rests the gun,
> And hang, in idle trophy, near,
> The game-pouch, fishing-rod, and spear;
> When wiry terrier, rough and grim,
> And greyhound, with his length of limb,
> And pointer, now employ'd no more,
> Cumber our parlour's narrow floor;
> When in his stall the impatient steed
> Is long condemn'd to rest and feed;
> When from our snow-encircled home
> Scarce cares the hardiest step to roam,
> Since path is none, save that to bring
> The needful water from the spring . . .
> When such the country cheer, I come
> Well pleas'd, to seek our city home.

In 1806 Scott gave up his practice at the Bar to become

one of the Clerks of Session, a position which required his presence in court three or four hours a day except in the vacation.

Scott's lease of Ashestiel expired in 1811. This gave him an excuse to satisfy one of his strongest and oldest ambitions—to become, like his ancestors, a land-owner by the banks of Tweed. He bought a farm of about a hundred acres near to Melrose, which he named Abbotsford. The actual moving of his goods and chattels took place in May 1812. "The neighbours have been much delighted," he wrote, "with the procession of my furniture, in which old swords, bows, targets, and lances made a very conspicuous show. A family of turkeys was accommodated within the helmet of some *preux chevalier* of ancient Border fame; and the very cows, for aught I know, were bearing banners and muskets." Scott was encouraged to buy the place by an increase in his salary as Clerk of Session and by the prospect of wealth from the sale of his books. But his first ideas were modest enough. He planned to build a cottage with a couple of spare bed-rooms for friends.

But Scott's ideas changed with his circumstances. A few years later he was earning more by his pen than any writer had ever done before in Britain. About 1805 he had written the first seven chapters of a novel, but after hearing a friend's unfavourable verdict he had thrown the manuscript aside into a desk. For a long while it was forgotten; later it was remembered, but he had forgotten where the papers were. At last in 1813, while searching out some fishing-tackle for a guest Scott came upon the manuscript, read it over, and wrote the rest of the story. This lucky chance proved a turning-point in his fortunes and produced the most famous series of historical novels in our language.

This story, *Waverley, or 'Tis Sixty Years Since*, appeared in 1814 without Scott's name. The secret of the authorship of this and the later novels, though known to some of Scott's closest friends, was not publicly acknowledged till 1827. The success of the books was immense. The stories by The Great Unknown, as he was called, were read throughout Europe and America. He could not write too quickly for the public. One, two, and sometimes even three novels appeared each year till the great creator's head and hand could do no more.

How Scott got his work done remains a wonder. He seemed no busier than the idlest of his guests at Abbotsford; he always had time for a ramble over the hills with his overseer, Tom Purdie, and the dogs. Tourists took up much of his time and occasionally ruffled even his easy temper. No one could have been less of an author in his habits. He could write a masterpiece in the midst of perpetual noise and bustle. *Guy Mannering*, one of his best books, was done in six weeks in the middle of Christmas celebrations. In the winter months in Edinburgh he was four hours a day in court and mixed much in general society. Yet with all this few days passed without a packet of manuscript being sent off to Ballantyne the printer.

One explanation of the ease of Scott's writing was that he had long been master of his subject. History, legend, and tradition had been his passion from boyhood. He had read for pleasure, and what is keenly enjoyed is not soon forgotten. He had stored his mind with the stuff of a hundred historical romances; he now began to use his riches. He wrote as quickly as his pen could travel, and what he wrote he seldom or never revised.

The sale of his books brought Scott about £10,000 a year. His first idea of building a simple cottage was forgotten, and a fortune was spent on a costly elaborate castle. He bought more and more land, and by 1816 his estate had grown to a thousand acres. It seemed to Scott and to Constable his publisher that his imagination was an inexhaustible gold-mine; that as long as the public would buy he could write. Scott was paid in advance for books of which he had not written even the titles.

Yet in spite of this worry of building operations and land-buying, and of tourists, the years at Abbotsford were rich in happiness and experience. No one loved and knew the countryside better than Scott, for whom every glen and hill had its tradition. He said that he would die if he did not see the heather once a year. No one was more popular with all ranks of men, from the Duke of Buccleuch, his neighbour and his family chief, down to the country folk who worked on the estate. Fame never destroyed Scott's simple geniality. Though he accepted a baronetcy and though his books were read and imitated everywhere he was never affected by vanity.

His health, however, was not so good, and for a couple of years he was troubled with violent cramps in the stomach. It was at this time, when tired and overtaxed, that he wrote his touching song, *The Dreary Change*.

> The sun upon the Weirdlaw Hill,
> In Ettrick's vale is sinking sweet;
> The westland wind is hush and still,
> The lake lies sleeping at my feet.
> Yet not the landscape to mine eye
> Bears those bright hues that once it bore;
> Though evening with her richest dye,
> Flames o'er the hills of Ettrick's shore.
>
> With listless look along the plain,
> I see Tweed's silver current glide,
> And coldly mark the holy fane
> Of Melrose rise in ruin'd pride.

The quiet lake, the balmy air,
The hill, the stream, the tower, the tree,—
Are they still such as once they were?
Or is the dreary change in me?

Alas, the warp'd and broken board,
How can it bear the painter's dye!
The harp of strain'd and tuneless chord,
How to the minstrel's skill reply!
To aching eyes each landscape lowers,
To feverish pulse each gale blows chill;
And Araby's or Eden's bowers
Were barren as this moorland hill.

But even when pain prevented his holding a pen he managed to dictate while he lay on a sofa. The greater part of *The Bride of Lammermoor* was produced in this way, and so severe had the strain been that when Scott saw the book after its publication he remembered nothing of what he had dictated. At no time in his life did he allow bodily suffering and weakness to have their own way and keep him from his work.

In January 1826 Scott's days of prosperity suddenly ended. Archibald Constable, the publisher, and James Ballantyne, the printer, of the Waverley Novels failed. For some years Scott had been Ballantyne's partner in the printing concern, and was now liable for the debts of the company which exceeded £100,000. Scott bore his reverses with quiet bravery. On the evening when the bad news was confirmed he dined with his old friend, James Skene, and appeared in his usual high spirits. On leaving he asked Skene to call on him the next morning, and was found seated at his writing-table busy with papers. He held out his hand to Skene, saying, "This is the hand of a beggar." But Scott wasted little time in regrets and melancholy. His main sorrow was for his wife and children. "For myself," he said, "I feel

like the Eildon Hills—quite firm, though a little cloudy."
He faced his situation with dogged heroism. Offers of
help poured in from every side, but he rejected them all.
"I will involve no friend, either rich or poor. My own
right hand shall do it." He trusted to his wonderful
pen to clear off the enormous debt. The brave sad story
of his courage and industry is told in his Journal which
he had begun to keep just before the crash. It is one
of the greatest records of proud endurance in our language; in many ways it is the greatest book Scott wrote.
The years of prosperity had not weakened Scott's
character. He showed himself at need a true descendant
of his fighting ancestors. But it was a fight against time.
Scott was no longer young; he was fifty-four, and his
busy life had told on him. He himself hardly expected
to live beyond sixty.

Scott turned at once to his task. When disaster came
he had a novel half written, and wrote a chapter on
each of the days which immediately followed. In
Edinburgh, when not in court, he wrought at his desk;
at Abbotsford his day's work was broken by a walk or
by helping Tom Purdie thin out the trees which they had
planted a dozen years before. Increasing lameness and
rheumatism had ended his days of long rambles and
venturesome rides. In spite of failing health and the
shock of his wife's death in May 1826, Scott paid off a
third of the debt between 1826 and 1828. In that time
he earned for his creditors nearly £40,000. "There is a
touch of the old spirit in me yet," he proudly declared,
"that bids me brave the tempest—the spirit that, in
spite of manifold infirmities, made me a roaring boy, in
my youth a desperate climber, a bold rider, and a stout
player at single-stick, of all which valuable qualities
there are now but slender remains."

The same monotonous toiling went on through 1829, but with increasing signs of breaking health and ebbing strength. His pleasure in Abbotsford was lessened by the death of Tom Purdie in October. "I think the woods will never look the same again," said Scott. But suffering of mind and body could not make him idle. The first of several paralytic strokes—"a shaking hands with death" Scott called it—occurred in February 1830, but he was not deterred from work. He merely took it as a sign that he must toil the harder if he was to clear himself of debt. All his ailments increased his old lameness, and it became hard for him to get enough exercise. It was obvious also to those near him that his mind was not what it had been. His wonderful memory sometimes betrayed him, he would lose the thread of a story, and words would no longer always obey him. "His strength was passing from him and he was becoming weak like unto other men." But with all this he wrote almost as much in 1830 as in 1829. When his doctors urged him to rest he told them they might just as well put a kettle on the fire and tell it not to boil.

In July 1831 he made an expedition with his son-in-law Lockhart to Douglas Castle and the neighbourhood, which he had not visited since boyhood. He wished to describe it in *Castle Dangerous*, a story he was then busy with, the last and not the worst of the Waverley Novels. On his journey home the news of an old friend's death seemed to him a warning that his own time was short. "I must home to work while it is called day," he said; "for the night cometh when no man can work. I put that text, many a year ago, on my dial-stone; but it often preached in vain."

Scott at last consented to try if rest and a milder climate would "make an old fellow of sixty young again."

Just before he left Abbotsford for Italy the poet Words-
worth arrived to bid him farewell and wrote his noble
poem:

> A trouble, not of clouds, or weeping rain,
> Nor of the setting sun's pathetic light
> Engendered, hangs o'er Eildon's triple height:
> Spirits of Power, assembled there, complain
> For kindred Power departing from their sight;
> While Tweed, best pleased in chanting a blithe strain.
> Saddens his voice again, and yet again.
> Lift up your hearts, ye Mourners! for the might
> Of the whole world's good wishes with him goes;
> Blessings and prayers in nobler retinue
> Than sceptred king or laurelled conqueror knows,
> Follow this wondrous Potentate. Be true,
> Ye winds of ocean, and the midland sea,
> Wafting your Charge to soft Parthenope!

On 29th October he set sail with his elder son and
younger daughter in a frigate placed at his disposal by
the Government. Even during the voyage and in spite of
the warnings of his doctors Scott took up his pen again.
Inactivity was impossible for him. From the first he had
struggled against circumstances, and he refused now to
be a passive invalid. The spirit of his life and of his
books is expressed in the lines:

> Sound, sound the clarion, fill the fife,
> To all the sensual world proclaim,—
> One crowded hour of glorious life
> Is worth an age without a name.

In the middle of December he reached Naples where he
spent his time in study, in writing and in expeditions to
famous places. But his thoughts were with his Border
land, and the Italian lakes and hills set songs about
"Charlie and his men" ringing in his head. He became

anxious and impatient to return to Scotland. After a
visit to Rome he turned homewards, travelling through
the Tyrol and Germany. He had no longer any hope
of recovery and did not wish to die abroad. "Let us
to Abbotsford," he exclaimed. Just before reaching
England (June 1832) he suffered another attack of
apoplexy and paralysis. For weeks he lay in a stupor in
London, though rousing himself at moments. His one
desire was for Abbotsford, and the doctors finally consented to his removal. As he caught sight of the familiar
sights by the Tweed he grew excited and threw off his
lethargy and could hardly be kept in the carriage. He
lingered on till 21st September, and died, as he had
wished, with the sounds of the rippling Tweed in
his ears.

Few writers have given more pleasure than Scott. His
books are crowded with interesting people of all sorts,
kings, queens, peasants, preachers. He filled the past
with living men and women. He makes us feel that
history is a stirring record of high deeds and great
characters. But if he was great as a writer he was greater
as a man. When George IV. visited Scotland in 1822 the
country at once put Scott forward as its representative.
Though literature brought Scott fame and wealth, he
always thought an author far inferior to a man who
played a part in the practical business of the world.
Few men who have been so widely known have been so
modest. When somebody praised him for the honour
and service he had done Scotland, he replied that he had
merely played the part of housemaid and given the country "a rubbing-up." He had hosts of friends; men and
women of all ranks from the King down to Tom Purdie
were won by his simplicity and generosity. Even in

his last years, when, as he said himself, he was pumping his brains for his creditors, he found time to help struggling authors with his pen. If Scott had never written a line he would deserve to be remembered as a great man. It is fortunate he has put so much of himself into his books.

The stories given here are from the *Tales of a Grandfather*. The book was made for John Hugh Lockhart, Sir Walter's first and favourite grandson. Before putting the tales down on paper he tried them on Hugh Littlejohn, as he liked to call him, to see if he understood and enjoyed them. He wished the lad to have the stories which had been the delight of his own boyhood. Scott had travelled the highroad and explored the bypaths of Scottish history ever since, as a youngster at Sandy Knowe, he had heard his grandmother tell of old Border heroes. To journey once again through the centuries from Wallace down to Prince Charles was a delight in spite of failing strength and heavy anxieties. Nothing could dull Scott's zest in the romance of his country's past.

Scott read the stories about Wallace in the old patriotic poem by Blind Harry. Bruce's adventures are told in the stirring poem by John Barbour written about half a century after Bannockburn. In Barbour too he found the exploits of Randolph and the good Sir James Douglas. On his visit to the ruined Castle of Douglas the year before his death Scott recited passages from Blind Harry and Barbour which had been ringing in his head since boyhood. The battle between the Percy and the Douglas is the subject of one of the most famous of Border ballads. Scott had the same feeling for it as Sir Philip Sidney had: "I never heard the old song of Percy and Douglas that I found not my heart moved more than with a trumpet." One stanza came to his lips at more than one serious moment in his life:

> My wound is deep; I fain would sleep;
> Take thou the vanguard of the three,
> And hide me by the bracken-bush
> That grows on yonder lily-lea.

The combat between the champions of Clan Chattan and Clan Kay is one of the most exciting incidents in Scott's novel *The Fair Maid of Perth*. The fondness of James V., the Goodman of Ballengiech, for wandering about in disguise had already been used by Scott in *The Lady of the Lake*. Scott had good reason to be interested in the rescue of Kinmont Willie, for it was an exploit of his ancestor and namesake Sir Walter Scott of Branxholm, laird of Buccleuch. The hero of the next story, *A Border Marriage*, was another of his ancestors, Sir William Scott. On a voyage to the Western Isles in 1814 Scott heard the grim tales of feuds and revenge which he tells here. He saw the bones of the MacDonalds in the cave and carried off a skull for his museum at Abbotsford. And lastly there is Prince Charles. The two Stuart rebellions of 1715 and 1745 had long been his darling subject. His great-grandfather had fought in the earlier rising and had nearly been hanged for it. Prince Charles is a gallant figure in *Waverley* and a pathetic one in *Redgauntlet*. "I became a valiant Jacobite at the age of ten years," Scott confessed, "and ever since reason and reading came to my assistance, I have never quite got rid of the impression which the gallantry of Prince Charles made on my imagination." His wanderings and escape after Culloden make one of the most romantic stories in history.

TALES OF A GRANDFATHER

SIR WILLIAM WALLACE

I. *The Barns of Ayr*

WILLIAM WALLACE was none of the high nobles of Scotland, but the son of a private gentleman, called Wallace of Ellerslie, in Renfrewshire, near Paisley. He was very tall and handsome, and one of the strongest and bravest that ever lived. He had a very fine countenance, with a quantity of fair hair, and was particularly dexterous in the use of all weapons which were then employed in battle. Wallace, like all Scotsmen of high spirit, had looked with great indignation upon the usurpation of the crown by Edward, and upon the insolences which the English soldiers committed on his countrymen. It is said, that when he was very young, he went a-fishing for sport in the river of Irvine, near Ayr. He had caught a good many trouts, which were carried by a boy, who attended him with a fishing-basket, as is usual with anglers. Two or three English soldiers who belonged to the garrison of Ayr came up to Wallace, and insisted, with their usual insolence, on taking the fish from the boy. Wallace was contented to allow them a part of the trouts, but he refused to part with the whole basketful. The soldiers insisted, and from words came to blows. Wallace had no better weapon than the butt-end of his fishing-rod; but he struck the foremost of the Englishmen so hard under the ear with it, that he killed him on the spot; and getting possession of the slain man's sword, he fought with so much fury that he put the others to flight, and brought home his fish safe and sound. The English governor of Ayr sought for him, to punish him with death for this action; but Wallace lay concealed among the hills and great woods till the matter was forgotten, and then appeared in another part of the country. He is said to have had other adventures of the same kind, in which he gallantly defended himself, sometimes when alone, sometimes with very few companions, against superior numbers of the English, until at last his name became generally known as a terror to them.

But the action which occasioned his finally rising in arms is believed to have happened in the town of Lanark. Wallace was at this time married to a lady of that place, and residing there with his wife. It chanced, as he walked in the market-place, dressed in a green garment, with a rich dagger by his side, that an Englishman came up and insulted him on account of his finery, saying, a Scotsman had no business to wear so gay a dress, or carry so handsome a weapon. It soon came to a quarrel, as on many former occasions; and Wallace, having killed the Englishman, fled to his own house, which was speedily assaulted by all the English soldiers. While they were endeavouring to force their way in at the front of the house Wallace escaped by a back-door, and got in safety to a rugged and rocky glen, near Lanark, called the Cartland crags, all covered with bushes and trees, and full of high precipices, where he knew he should be safe from the pursuit of the English soldiers. In the meantime the governor of Lanark, whose name was Hazelrigg, burned Wallace's house, and put

his wife and servants to death; and by committing this
cruelty increased to the highest pitch, as you may well believe, the hatred which the champion had always borne
against the English usurper. Hazelrigg also proclaimed
Wallace an outlaw, and offered a reward to any one who
should bring him to an English garrison, alive or dead.

On the other hand, Wallace soon collected a body of
men, outlawed like himself, or willing to become so, rather
than any longer endure the oppression of the English.
One of his earliest expeditions was directed against
Hazelrigg, whom he killed, and thus avenged the death
of his wife. He fought skirmishes with the soldiers who
were sent against him, and often defeated them; and in
time became so well known and so formidable that
multitudes began to resort to his standard, until at
length he was at the head of a considerable army,
with which he proposed to restore his country to
independence.

About this time is said to have taken place a memorable event, which the Scottish people called the *Barns of
Ayr*. It is alleged that the English governor of Ayr had
invited the greater part of the Scottish nobility and
gentry in the western parts to meet him at some large
buildings called the Barns of Ayr, for the purpose of
friendly conference upon the affairs of the nation. But
the English earl entertained the treacherous purpose of
putting the Scottish gentlemen to death. The English
soldiers had halters with running nooses ready prepared,
and hung upon the beams which supported the roof;
and, as the Scottish gentlemen were admitted by two
and two at a time, the nooses were thrown over their
heads, and they were pulled up by the neck, and thus
hanged or strangled to death. Among those who were
slain in this base and treacherous manner was, it is said,

Sir Reginald Crawford, Sheriff of the county of Ayr, and uncle to William Wallace.

When Wallace heard of what had befallen he was dreadfully enraged, and collecting his men in a wood near the town of Ayr, he resolved to be revenged on the authors of this great crime. The English in the meanwhile made much feasting, and when they had eaten and drunk plentifully, they lay down to sleep in the same large barns in which they had murdered the Scottish gentlemen. But Wallace, learning that they kept no guard or watch, not suspecting there were any enemies so near them, directed a woman who knew the place to mark with chalk the doors of the lodgings where the Englishmen lay. Then he sent a party of men, who, with strong ropes, made all the doors so fast on the outside that those within could not open them. On the outside the Scots had prepared heaps of straw, to which they set fire, and the Barns of Ayr, being themselves made of wood, were soon burning in a bright flame. Then the English were awakened, and endeavoured to get out to save their lives. But the doors, as I told you, were secured on the outside, and bound fast with ropes; and, besides, the blazing houses were surrounded by the Scots, who forced those who got out to run back into the fire, or else put them to death on the spot; and thus great numbers perished miserably. Many of the English were lodged in a convent, but they had no better fortune than the others; for the prior of the convent caused all the friars to arm themselves, and, attacking the English guests, they put most of them to the sword. This was called the "Friar of Ayr's blessing." We cannot tell if this story of the *Barns of Ayr* be exactly true; but it is probable there is some foundation for it, as it is universally believed in that country.

II. *Stirling Bridge*

Thus Wallace's party grew daily stronger and stronger, and many of the Scottish nobles joined with him. Among these were Sir William Douglas, the Lord of Douglas-Dale, and the head of a great family often mentioned in Scottish history. There was also Sir John the Grahame, who became Wallace's bosom friend and greatest confidant. Many of these great noblemen, however, deserted the cause of the country on the approach of John de Warenne, Earl of Surrey, the English governor, at the head of a numerous and well-appointed army. They thought that Wallace would be unable to withstand the attack of so many disciplined soldiers, and hastened to submit themselves to the English, for fear of losing their estates. Wallace, however, remained undismayed, and at the head of a considerable army. He had taken up his camp upon the northern side of the river Forth, near the town of Stirling. The river was there crossed by a long wooden bridge, about a mile above the spot where the present bridge is situated.

The English general approached the banks of the river on the southern side. He sent two clergymen to offer a pardon to Wallace and his followers, on condition that they should lay down their arms. But such was not the purpose of the high-minded champion of Scotland.

"Go back to Warenne," said Wallace, "and tell him we value not the pardon of the King of England. We are not here for the purpose of treating of peace, but of abiding battle, and restoring freedom to our country. Let the English come on;—we defy them to their very beards!"

The English, upon hearing this haughty answer, called loudly to be led to the attack. Their leader, Sir Richard Lundin, a Scottish knight, who had gone over to the enemy at Irvine, hesitated, for he was a skilful soldier, and he saw that, to approach the Scottish army, his troops must pass over the long, narrow wooden bridge; so that those who should get over first might be attacked by Wallace with all his forces, before those who remained behind could possibly come to their assistance. He therefore inclined to delay the battle. But Cressingham the treasurer, who was ignorant and presumptuous, insisted that it was their duty to fight, and put an end to the war at once; and Lundin gave way to his opinion, although Cressingham, being a churchman, could not be so good a judge of what was fitting as he himself, an experienced officer.

The English army began to cross the bridge, Cressingham leading the van, or foremost division of the army; for in those military days, even clergymen wore armour and fought in battle. That took place which Lundin had foreseen. Wallace suffered a considerable part of the English army to pass the bridge, without offering any opposition; but when about one-half were over, and the bridge was crowded with those who were following, he charged those who had crossed with his whole strength, slew a very great number, and drove the rest into the river Forth, where the greater part were drowned. The remainder of the English army, who were left on the southern bank of the river, fled in great confusion, having first set fire to the wooden bridge that the Scots might not pursue them. Cressingham was killed in the very beginning of the battle; and the Scots detested him so much, that they flayed the skin from his dead body, and kept pieces of it, in memory of the revenge they had taken upon the English treasurer. Some say they made saddle-girths of this same skin; a purpose for which I do not think it could be very fit. It must be owned to have been a dishonourable thing of the Scots to insult thus the dead body of their enemy, and shows that they must have been then a ferocious and barbarous people.

The remains of Surrey's great army fled out of Scotland after this defeat; and the Scots, taking arms on all sides, attacked the castles in which the English soldiers continued to shelter themselves, and took most of them by force or stratagem. Many wonderful stories are told of Wallace's exploits on these occasions; some of which are no doubt true, while others are either invented, or very much exaggerated. It seems certain, however, that he defeated the English in several combats, chased them almost entirely out of Scotland, regained the towns and castles of which they had possessed themselves, and recovered for a time the complete freedom of the country. He even marched into England, and laid Cumberland and Northumberland waste, where the Scottish soldiers, in revenge for the mischief which the English had done in their country, committed great cruelties. Wallace did not approve of their killing the people who were not in arms, and he endeavoured to protect the clergymen and others, who were not able to defend themselves. "Remain with me," he said to the priests of Hexham, a large town in Northumberland, "for I cannot protect you from my soldiers when you are out of my presence." The troops who followed Wallace received no pay, because he had no money to give them; and that was one great reason why he could not keep them under restraint, or prevent their doing much harm to the defenceless country people. He remained in England more than three weeks, and did a great deal of mischief to the country.

Indeed, it appears that, though Wallace disapproved of slaying priests, women, and children, he partook of the ferocity of the times so much as to put to death

B

without quarter all whom he found in arms. In the
north of Scotland, the English had placed a garrison in
the strong castle of Dunnottar, which, built on a large
and precipitous rock, overhangs the raging sea. Though
the place is almost inaccessible, Wallace and his soldiers
found their way into the castle, while the garrison in
great terror fled into the church or chapel, which was
built on the very verge of the precipice. This did not save
them, for Wallace caused the church to be set on fire.
The terrified garrison, involved in the flames, ran, some
of them, upon the points of the Scottish swords, while
others threw themselves from the precipice into the sea,
and swam along to the cliffs, where they hung like sea-
fowl, screaming in vain for mercy and assistance.

The followers of Wallace were frightened at this
dreadful scene, and falling on their knees before the
priests who chanced to be in the army, they asked
forgiveness for having committed so much slaughter
within the limits of a church dedicated to the service of
God. But Wallace had so deep a sense of the injuries
which the English had done to his country, that he only
laughed at the contrition of his soldiers—"I will absolve
you all myself," he said. "Are you Scottish soldiers,
and do you repent for a trifle like this, which is not half
what the invaders deserved at our hands?" So deep-
seated was Wallace's feeling of national resentment,
that it seems to have overcome, in such instances, the
scruples of a temper which was naturally humane.

III. *The Battle of Falkirk and Death of Wallace.*

Edward I. was in Flanders when all these events
took place. You may suppose he was very angry when
he learned that Scotland, which he thought completely
subdued, had risen into a great insurrection against him,

defeated his armies, killed his treasurer, chased his soldiers out of their country, and invaded England with a great force. He came back from Flanders in a mighty rage, and determined not to leave that rebellious country until it was finally conquered; for which purpose he assembled a very fine army, and marched into Scotland.

In the meantime the Scots prepared to defend themselves, and chose Wallace to be Governor or Protector of the kingdom, because they had no king at the time. He was now titled Sir William Wallace, Protector or Governor of the Scottish nation. But although Wallace, as we have seen, was the best soldier and bravest man in Scotland, and therefore the most fit to be placed in command at this critical period, when the king of England was coming against them with such great forces, yet the nobles of Scotland envied him this important situation, because he was not a man born in high rank, or enjoying a large estate. So great was their jealousy of Sir William Wallace, that many of these great barons did not seem very willing to bring forward their forces, or fight against the English, because they would not have a man of inferior condition to be general. This was base and mean conduct, and it was attended with great disasters to Scotland. Yet, notwithstanding this unwillingness of the great nobility to support him, Wallace assembled a large army; for the middling, but especially the lower classes, were very much attached to him. He marched boldly against the king of England, and met him near the town of Falkirk. Most of the Scottish army were on foot, because, as I already told you, in those days only the nobility and great men of Scotland fought on horseback. The English king, on the contrary, had a very large body of the finest cavalry in the world, Normans and English, all clothed in complete armour. He had also the celebrated archers of England, each of whom was said to carry twelve Scotsmen's lives under his girdle; because every archer had twelve arrows stuck in his belt, and was expected to kill a man with every arrow.

The Scots had some good archers from the Forest of Ettrick, who fought under command of Sir John Stewart of Bonkill; but they were not nearly equal in number to the English. The greater part of the Scottish army were on foot, armed with long spears; they were placed thick and close together, and laid all their spears so close, point over point, that it seemed as difficult to break through them as through the wall of a strong castle. When the two armies were drawn up facing each other, Wallace said to his soldiers, "I have brought you to the ring, let me see how you can dance"; meaning, I have brought you to the decisive field of battle, let me see how bravely you can fight.

The English made the attack. King Edward, though he saw the close ranks and undaunted appearance of the Scottish infantry, resolved nevertheless to try whether he could not ride them down with his fine cavalry. He therefore gave his horsemen orders to advance. They charged accordingly, at full gallop. It must have been a terrible thing to have seen these fine horses riding as hard as they could against the long lances, which were held out by the Scots to keep them back; and a dreadful cry arose when they came against each other.

The first line of cavalry was commanded by the Earl Marshal of England, whose progress was checked by a morass. The second line of English horse was commanded by Antony Beck, the Bishop of Durham, who, nevertheless, wore armour, and fought like a lay baron. He wheeled round the morass; but when he saw the deep and firm order of the Scots, his heart failed, and he proposed to Sir Ralph Basset of Drayton, who commanded under him, to halt till Edward himself brought up the reserve. "Go, say your mass, bishop," answered Basset contemptuously, and advanced at full gallop with the second line. However, the Scots stood their ground with their long spears; many of the foremost of the English horses were thrown down, and the riders were killed as they lay rolling, unable to rise, owing to the weight of their heavy armour. But the Scottish horse did not come to the assistance of their infantry, but, on the contrary, fled away from the battle. It is supposed that this was owing to the treachery or ill-will of the nobility, who were jealous of Wallace. But it must be considered that the Scottish cavalry were few in number; and that they had much worse arms, and weaker horses, than their enemies. The English cavalry attempted again and again to disperse the deep and solid ranks in which Wallace had stationed his foot soldiers. But they were repeatedly beaten off with loss, nor could they make their way through that wood of spears, as it is called by one of the English historians. King Edward then commanded his archers to advance; and these approaching within arrow-shot of the Scottish ranks, poured on them such close and dreadful volleys of arrows that it was impossible to sustain the discharge. It happened at the same time, that Sir John Stewart was killed by a fall from his horse; and the archers of Ettrick Forest, whom he was bringing forward to oppose those of King Edward, were slain in great numbers around him. Their bodies were afterwards distinguished among the slain, as being the tallest and handsomest men of the army.

The Scottish spearmen being thus thrown into some degree of confusion, by the loss of those who were slain by the arrows of the English, the heavy cavalry of Edward again charged with more success than formerly, and broke through the ranks, which were already disordered. Sir John Grahame, Wallace's great friend and companion, was slain, with many other brave soldiers; and the Scots, having lost a very great number of men, were at length obliged to take to flight.

This fatal battle was fought upon 22nd July, 1298. Sir John the Grahame lies buried in the churchyard of Falkirk. A tombstone was laid over him, which has been three times renewed since his death. The inscription bears, "That Sir John the Grahame, equally remarkable for wisdom and courage, and the faithful friend of Wallace, being slain in battle by the English, lies buried in this place." A large oak-tree in the adjoining forest was long shown as marking the spot where Wallace slept before the battle, or, as others said, in which he hid himself after the defeat. Nearly forty years ago Grandpapa saw some of its roots; but the body of the tree was even then entirely decayed, and there is not now, and has not been for many years, the least vestige of it to be seen.

After this fatal defeat of Falkirk, Sir William Wallace seems to have resigned his office of Governor of Scotland. Several nobles were named guardians in his place, and continued to make resistance to the English armies. . . . Nevertheless, the king of England possessed so much wealth, and so many means of raising soldiers, that he sent army after army into the poor oppressed country of Scotland, and obliged all its nobles and great men, one after another, to submit themselves once more to his yoke. Sir William Wallace, alone, or with a very small band of followers, refused either to acknowledge the usurper Edward or to lay down his arms. He continued to maintain himself among the woods and mountains of his native country for no less than seven years after his defeat at Falkirk, and for more than one year after all the other defenders of Scottish liberty had laid down their arms. Many proclamations were sent out against him by the English, and a great reward was set upon his head; for Edward did not think he could have any secure possession of his usurped kingdom of Scotland while Wallace lived. At length he was taken prisoner; and, shame it is to say, a Scotsman, called Sir John Menteith, was the person by whom he was seized and delivered to the English. It is generally said that he was made prisoner at Robroyston, near Glasgow; and the tradition of the country bears that the signal made for rushing upon him and taking him at unawares was, when one of his pretended friends, who betrayed him, should turn a loaf, which was placed upon the table, with its bottom or flat side uppermost. And in after times it was reckoned ill-breeding to turn a loaf in that manner if there was a person named Menteith in company; since it was as much as to remind him that his namesake had betrayed Sir William Wallace, the Champion of Scotland.

Whether Sir John Menteith was actually the person by whom Wallace was betrayed is not perfectly certain. He was, however, the individual by whom the patriot was made prisoner and delivered up to the English, for which his name and his memory have been long loaded with disgrace.

Edward having thus obtained possession of the person whom he considered as the greatest obstacle to his complete conquest of Scotland, resolved to make Wallace an example to all Scottish patriots who should in future venture to oppose his ambitious projects. He caused this gallant defender of his country to be brought to trial in Westminster Hall, before the English judges, and produced him there, crowned, in mockery, with a green garland, because they said he had been king of outlaws and robbers among the Scottish woods. Wallace was accused of having been a traitor to the English crown; to which he answered, "I could not be a traitor to Edward, for I was never his subject." He was then charged with having taken and burnt towns and castles, with having killed many men and done much violence. He replied with the same calm resolution, "That it was true he had killed very many Englishmen, but it was because they had come to subdue and oppress his native country of Scotland; and far from repenting what he had done, he declared he was only sorry that he had not put to death many more of them."

Notwithstanding that Wallace's defence was a good one, both in law and in common sense (for surely every one has not only a right to fight in defence of his native country, but is bound in duty to do so), the English judges condemned him to be executed. So this brave patriot was dragged upon a sledge to the place of execution, where his head was struck off, and his body divided into four quarters, which, according to the cruel custom of the time, were exposed upon spikes of iron on London Bridge, and were termed the limbs of a traitor.

No doubt King Edward thought, that by exercising this great severity towards so distinguished a patriot as Sir William Wallace he should terrify all the Scots into obedience, and so be able in future to reign over their country without resistance. But though Edward was a powerful, a brave, and a wise king, and though he took the most cautious, as well as the most strict measures, to preserve the obedience of Scotland, yet his claim being founded in injustice and usurpation, was not permitted by Providence to be established in security or peace. Sir William Wallace, that immortal supporter of the independence of his country, was no sooner deprived of his life, in the cruel and unjust manner I have told you, than other patriots arose to assert the cause of Scottish liberty.

ADVENTURES OF ROBERT BRUCE

I. *The Red Comyn.*

Now, this Robert the Bruce was a remarkably brave and strong man: there was no man in Scotland that was thought a match for him except Sir William Wallace; and now that Wallace was dead, Bruce was held the best warrior in Scotland. He was very wise and prudent, and an excellent general: that is, he knew how to conduct an army, and place them in order for battle, as well or better than any great man of his time. He was generous, too, and courteous by nature; but he had some faults, which perhaps belonged as much to the fierce period in which he lived as to his own character. He was rash and passionate, and in his passion he was sometimes relentless and cruel.

Robert the Bruce had fixed his purpose, as I told you, to attempt once again to drive the English out of Scotland, and he desired to prevail upon Sir John the Red Comyn, who was his rival in his pretensions to the throne, to join with him in expelling the foreign enemy by their common efforts. With this purpose, Bruce posted down from London to Dumfries, on the borders of Scotland, and requested an interview with John Comyn. They met in the church of the Minorites in that town, before the high altar. What passed betwixt them is not known with certainty; but they quarrelled, either concerning their mutual pretensions to the crown, or because Comyn refused to join Bruce in the proposed insurrection against the English; or, as many writers say, because Bruce charged Comyn with having betrayed

to the English his purpose of rising up against King
Edward. It is, however, certain that these two haughty
barons came to high and abusive words, until at length
Bruce, who, I told you, was extremely passionate, forgot
the sacred character of the place in which they stood,
and struck Comyn a blow with his dagger. Having done
this rash deed, he instantly ran out of the church and
called for his horse. Two gentlemen of the country,
Lindesay and Kirkpatrick, friends of Bruce, were then
in attendance on him. Seeing him pale, bloody, and
in much agitation, they eagerly inquired what was
the matter.

"I doubt," said Bruce, "that I have slain the Red
Comyn."

"Do you leave such a matter in doubt?" said Kirkpatrick. "I will make sicker!"—that is, I will make certain.

Accordingly, he and his companion Lindesay rushed
into the church and made the matter certain with a
vengeance, by despatching the wounded Comyn with
their daggers. His uncle, Sir Robert Comyn, was slain at
the same time.

This slaughter of Comyn was a rash and cruel action;
and the historian of Bruce observes that it was followed
by the displeasure of Heaven; for no man ever went
through more misfortunes than Robert Bruce, although
he at length rose to great honour.

After the deed was done, Bruce might be called desperate. He had committed an action which was sure to
bring down upon him the vengeance of all Comyn's
relations, the resentment of the king of England, and
the displeasure of the Church, on account of having
slain his enemy within consecrated ground. He determined, therefore, to bid them all defiance at once, and
to assert his pretensions to the throne of Scotland. He

drew his own followers together, summoned to meet him such barons as still entertained hopes of the freedom of the country, and was crowned King at the Abbey of Scone, the usual place where the kings of Scotland assumed their authority.

Everything relating to the ceremony was hastily performed. A small circlet of gold was hurriedly made, to represent the ancient crown of Scotland, which Edward had carried off to England. The Earl of Fife, descendant of the brave Macduff, whose duty it was to have placed the crown on the king's head, would not give his attendance. But the ceremonial was performed by his sister, Isabella, Countess of Buchan, though without the consent either of her brother or husband. A few barons, whose names ought to be dear to their country, joined Bruce in his attempt to vindicate the independence of Scotland.

Edward was dreadfully incensed when he heard that, after all the pains which he had taken, and all the blood which had been spilled, the Scots were making this new attempt to shake off his authority. Though now old, feeble, and sickly, he made a solemn vow, at a great festival, in the presence of all his court, that he would take the most ample vengeance upon Robert the Bruce and his adherents; after which he would only fight against the unbelieving Saracens for the recovery of the Holy Land. He marched against Bruce accordingly, at the head of a powerful army.

The commencement of Bruce's undertaking was most disastrous. He was crowned on 29th March, 1306. On the 18th May he was excommunicated by the Pope, on account of the murder of Comyn within consecrated ground, a sentence which excluded him from all the benefits of religion, and authorised any one to kill him. Finally, on the 19th June, the new king was completely defeated near Methven by the English Earl of Pembroke. Robert's horse was killed under him in the action, and he was for a moment a prisoner. But he had fallen into the power of a Scottish knight, who, though he served in the English army, did not choose to be the instrument of putting Bruce into their hands, and allowed him to escape. The conquerors executed their prisoners with their usual cruelty. Among these were some gallant young men of the first Scottish families—Hay, ancestor of the Earls of Errol, Somerville, Fraser, and others who were mercilessly put to death.

II. *The Brooch of Lorn.*

Bruce, with a few brave adherents, among whom was the young Lord of Douglas, who was afterwards called the Good Lord James, retired into the Highland mountains, where they were chased from one place of refuge to another, often in great danger, and suffering many hardships. The Bruce's wife, now Queen of Scotland, with several other ladies, accompanied her husband and his few followers during their wanderings. There was no other way of providing for them save by hunting and fishing. It was remarked that Douglas was the most active and successful in procuring for the unfortunate ladies such supplies as his dexterity in fishing or in killing deer could furnish them.

Driven from one place in the Highlands to another, starved out of some districts, and forced from others by the opposition of the inhabitants, Bruce attempted to force his way into Lorn; but he found enemies everywhere. The M'Dougals, a powerful family, then called Lords of Lorn, were friendly to the English, and putting their men in arms, attacked Bruce and his wandering companions as soon as they attempted to enter their territory. The chief of these M'Dougals, called John of Lorn, hated Bruce on account of his having slain the Red Comyn, to whom this M'Dougal was nearly related. Bruce was again defeated by this chief, through force of numbers, at a place called Dalry; but he showed, amidst his misfortunes, the greatness of his strength and courage. He directed his men to retreat through a narrow pass, and placing himself last of the party, he fought with and slew such of the enemy as attempted to press hard on them. Three followers of M'Dougal, a father and two sons called M'Androsser, all very strong men, when they saw Bruce thus protecting the retreat of his followers, made a vow that they would either kill this redoubted champion or make him prisoner. The whole three rushed on the king at once. Bruce was on horseback, in the strait pass we have described, betwixt a precipitous rock and a deep lake. He struck the first man who came up, and seized his horse's rein, such a blow with his sword, as cut off his hand and freed the bridle. The man bled to death. The other brother had grasped Bruce in the meantime by the leg, and was attempting to throw him from horseback. The king, setting spurs to his horse, made the animal suddenly spring forward, so that the Highlander fell under the horse's feet; and, as he was endeavouring to rise again, Bruce cleft his head in two with his sword. The father, seeing his two sons thus slain, flew desperately at the king, and grasped him by the mantle so close to his body, that he could not have room to wield his long sword. But with the heavy pommel of that weapon, or, as others say, with an iron hammer which hung at his saddle-bow, the king struck this third assailant so dreadful a blow that he dashed out his brains. Still, however, the Highlander kept his dying grasp on the king's mantle; so that, to be free of the dead body,

Bruce was obliged to undo the brooch, or clasp, by which it was fastened, and leave that, and the mantle itself, behind him. The brooch which fell thus into the possession of M'Dougal of Lorn, is still preserved in that ancient family, as a memorial that the celebrated Robert Bruce once narrowly escaped falling into the hands of their ancestor. Robert greatly resented this attack upon him: and when he was in happier circumstances, did not fail to take his revenge on M'Dougal or, as he is usually called, John of Lorn. . . .

III. *The Three Traitors.*

At one time a near relation of Bruce's, in whom he entirely confided, was induced by the bribes of the English to attempt to put him to death. This villain, with his two sons, watched the king one morning, till he saw him separated from all his men, excepting a little boy, who waited on him as a page. The father had a sword in his hand, one of the sons had a sword and a spear, the other had a sword and a battle-axe. Now, when the king saw them so well armed, when there were no enemies near, he began to call to mind some hints which had been given to him, that these men intended to murder him. He had no weapons excepting his sword; but his page had a bow and arrow. He took them both from the little boy, and bade him stand at a distance; "for," said the king, "if I overcome these traitors, thou shalt have enough of weapons; but if I am slain by them, you may make your escape, and tell Douglas and my brother to revenge my death." The boy was very sorry, for he loved his master; but he was obliged to do as he was bidden.

In the meantime the traitors came forward upon Bruce, that they might assault him at once. The king called out to them, and commanded them to come no

nearer, upon peril of their lives; but the father answered
with flattering words, pretending great kindness, and still
continuing to approach his person. Then the king again
called to them to stand. "Traitors," said he, "ye have
sold my life for English gold; but you shall die if you
come one foot nearer to me." With that he bent the page's
bow; and as the old conspirator continued to advance,
he let the arrow fly at him. Bruce was an excellent archer;
he aimed his arrow so well that it hit the father in the
eye, and penetrated from that into his brain, so that he
fell down dead. Then the two sons rushed on the king.
One of them fetched a blow at him with an axe,
but missed his stroke and stumbled, so that the king
with his great sword cut him down before he could
recover his feet. The remaining traitor ran on Bruce
with his spear; but the king, with a sweep of his
sword, cut the steel head off the villain's weapon, and
then killed him before he had time to draw his sword.
Then the little page came running, very joyful of his
master's victory; and the king wiped his bloody sword,
and looking upon the dead bodies, said, "These might
have been reputed three gallant men, if they could have
resisted the temptation of covetousness." . . .

IV. *The Fight at the Ford.*

After the death of these three traitors, Robert the
Bruce continued to keep himself concealed in his own
earldom of Carrick, and in the neighbouring country
of Galloway, until he should have matters ready for a
general attack upon the English. He was obliged, in
the meantime, to keep very few men with him, both for
the sake of secrecy, and from the difficulty of finding
provisions. Now, many of the people of Galloway were
unfriendly to Bruce. They lived under the government

of one M'Dougal, related to the Lord of Lorn. . . .
These Galloway men had heard that Bruce was in their
country, having no more than sixty men with him; so
they resolved to attack him by surprise, and for this
purpose they got two hundred men together, and brought
with them two or three bloodhounds. These animals
were trained to chase a man by the scent of his footsteps,
as foxhounds chase a fox, or as beagles and harriers
chase a hare. Although the dog does not see the person
whose trace he is put upon, he follows him over every
step he has taken. At that time these bloodhounds or
sleuthhounds (so called from *slot* or *sleut*, a word which
signifies the scent left by an animal of chase) were used
for the purpose of pursuing great criminals. The men of
Galloway thought themselves secure, that if they missed
taking Bruce, or killing him at the first onset, and if he
should escape into the woods, they would find him out
by means of these bloodhounds.

The good King Robert Bruce, who was always watchful
and vigilant, had received some information of the intention of this party to come upon him suddenly and by
night. Accordingly he quartered his little troop of sixty
men on the side of a deep and swift-running river, that
had very steep and rocky banks. There was but one ford
by which this river could be crossed in that neighbourhood,
and that ford was deep and narrow, so that two men could
scarcely get through abreast; the ground on which they
were to land on the side where the king was was steep,
and the path which led upwards from the water's edge to
the top of the bank extremely narrow and difficult.

Bruce caused his men to lie down to take some sleep,
at a place about half a mile distant from the river, while
he himself, with two attendants, went down to watch
the ford, through which the enemy must needs pass

before they could come to the place where King Robert's men were lying. He stood for some time looking at the ford, and thinking how easily the enemy might be kept from passing there, providing it was bravely defended, when he heard at a distance the baying of a hound, which was always coming nearer and nearer. This was the blood-hound which was tracing the king's steps to the ford where he had crossed, and the two hundred Galloway men were along with the animal, and guided by it. Bruce at first thought of going back to awaken his men; but then he reflected that it might be only some shepherd's dog. "My men," he said, "are sorely tired; I will not disturb their sleep for the yelping of a cur, till I know something more of the matter." So he stood and listened; and by and by, as the cry of the hound came nearer, he began to hear a trampling of horses and the voices of men, and the ringing and clattering of armour, and then he was sure the enemy were coming to the riverside. Then the king thought, "If I go back to give my men the alarm, these Galloway men will get through the ford without opposition; and that would be a pity, since it is a place so advantageous to make defence against them." So he looked again at the steep path and the deep river, and he thought that they gave him so much advantage that he himself could defend the passage with his own hand until his men came to assist him. His armour was so good and strong that he had no fear of arrows, and therefore the combat was not so very unequal as it must have otherwise been. He therefore sent his followers to waken his men, and remained alone by the bank of the river.

In the meanwhile, the noise and trampling of the horses increased; and the moon being bright, Bruce beheld the glancing arms of about two hundred men, who came down to the opposite bank of the river. The men of

Galloway, on their part, saw but one solitary figure, guarding the ford, and the foremost of them plunged into the river without minding him. But as they could only pass the ford one by one, the Bruce, who stood high above them on the bank where they were to land, killed the foremost man with a thrust of his long spear, and with a second thrust stabbed the horse, which fell down, kicking and plunging in his agonies, on the narrow path, and so prevented the others who were following from getting out of the river. Bruce had thus an opportunity of dealing his blows at pleasure among them, while they could not strike at him again. In the confusion, five or six of the enemy were slain, or, having been borne down the current, were drowned in the river. The rest were terrified, and drew back.

But when the Galloway men looked again, and saw they were opposed by only one man, they themselves being so many, they cried out that their honour would be lost for ever if they did not force their way; and encouraged each other with loud cries to plunge through and assault him. But by this time the king's soldiers came up to his assistance, and the Galloway men retreated, and gave up their enterprise.

V. *Bruce and the Bloodhound*

I will tell you another story of this brave Robert Bruce during his wanderings. His adventures are as curious and entertaining as those which men invent for story books, with this advantage, that they are all true.

About the time when the Bruce was yet at the head of but few men, Sir Aymer de Valence, who was Earl of Pembroke, together with John of Lorn, came into Galloway, each of them being at the head of a large body of men. John of Lorn had a bloodhound with him, which it was said had formerly belonged to Robert Bruce himself; and having been fed by the king with his own hands, it became attached to him, and would follow his footsteps anywhere, as dogs are well known to trace their master's steps, whether they be bloodhounds or not. By means of this hound, John of Lorn thought he should certainly find out Bruce, and take revenge on him for the death of his relation Comyn.

When these two armies advanced upon King Robert, he at first thought of fighting with the English earl; but becoming aware that John of Lorn was moving round with another large body to attack him in the rear, he resolved to avoid fighting at that time, lest he should be oppressed by numbers. For this purpose, the king divided the men he had with him into three bodies, and commanded them to retreat by three different ways, thinking the enemy would not know which party to pursue. He also appointed a place at which they were to assemble again. But when John of Lorn came to the place where the army of Bruce had been thus divided, the bloodhound took his course after one of these divisions, neglecting the other two, and then John of Lorn knew that the king must be in that party; so he also made no pursuit after the two other divisions of the Scots, but followed that which the dog pointed out, with all his men.

The king again saw that he was followed by a large body, and being determined to escape from them, if possible, he made all the people who were with him disperse themselves different ways, thinking thus that the enemy must needs lose trace of him. He kept only one man along with him, and that was his own foster-brother, or the son of his nurse. When John of Lorn came to the place where Bruce's companions had dispersed themselves, the bloodhound, after it had snuffed up and down for a little, quitted the footsteps of all the other fugitives, and ran barking upon the track of two men out of the whole number. Then John of Lorn knew that one of these two must needs be King Robert. Accordingly he commanded five of his men that were speedy of foot to follow hard, and either make him prisoner or slay him. The Highlanders started off accordingly, and ran so fast that they gained sight of Robert and his foster-brother. The king asked his companion what help he could give him, and his foster-brother answered he was ready to do his best. So these two turned on the five men of John of Lorn, and killed them all. It is to be supposed they were better armed than the others were, as well as stronger and more desperate.

But by this time Bruce was very much fatigued, and yet they dared not sit down to take any rest; for whenever they stopped for an instant, they heard the cry of the blood-hound behind them, and knew by that that their enemies were coming up fast after them. At length they came to a wood, through which ran a small river. The Bruce said to his foster-brother, "Let us wade down this stream for a great way, instead of going straight across, and so this unhappy hound will lose the scent; for if we were once clear of him, I should not be afraid of getting away from the pursuers." Accordingly the king and his attendant walked a great way down the stream, taking care to keep their feet in the water, which could not retain any scent where they had stepped. Then they came ashore on the further side from the enemy, and went deep into the wood before they stopped to rest themselves. In the meanwhile, the hound led John of Lorn straight to the place where the king went into the water, but there the dog began to be puzzled, not knowing where to go next; for you are well aware that the running water could not retain the scent of a man's foot, like that which remains on turf. So John of Lorn seeing the dog was at fault, as it is called, that is, had lost the track of what he pursued, gave up the chase, and returned to join with Aymer de Valence.

But King Robert's adventures were not yet ended. His foster-brother and he had rested themselves in the wood, but they had got no food, and were become extremely hungry. They walked on, however, in hopes of coming to some habitation. At length, in the midst of the forest, they met with three men who looked like thieves or ruffians. They were well armed, and one of them bore a sheep on his back, which it seemed as if they had just stolen. They saluted the king civilly; and he, replying to their salutation, asked them where they were going. The men answered, they were seeking for Robert Bruce, for that they intended to join with him. The king answered, that if they would go with him, he would conduct them where they would find the Scottish king. Then the man who had spoken changed countenance, and Bruce, who looked sharply at him, began to suspect that the ruffian guessed who he was, and that he and his companions had some design against his person, in order to gain the reward which had been offered for his life.

So he said to them, "My good friends, as we are not well acquainted with each other, you must go before us, and we will follow near to you."

"You have no occasion to suspect any harm from us," answered the man.

"Neither do I suspect any," said Bruce; "but this is the way in which I choose to travel."

The men did as he commanded, and thus they travelled till they came together to a waste and ruinous cottage, where the men proposed to dress some part of the sheep, which their companion was carrying. The king was glad to hear of food; but he insisted that there should be two fires kindled, one for himself and his foster-brother at one end of the house, the other at the other end for their three companions. The men did as he desired. They broiled a quarter of mutton for themselves, and gave another to the king and his attendant.

They were obliged to eat it without bread or salt; but as they were very hungry, they were glad to get food in any shape, and partook of it very heartily.

Then so heavy a drowsiness fell on King Robert, that, for all the danger he was in, he could not resist an inclination to sleep. But first he desired his foster-brother to watch while he slept, for he had great suspicion of their new acquaintances. His foster-brother promised to keep awake, and did his best to keep his word. But the king had not been long asleep ere his foster-brother fell into a deep slumber also, for he had undergone as much fatigue as the king. When the three villains saw the king and his attendant asleep, they made signs to each other, and rising up at once, drew their swords with the purpose to kill them both. But the king slept but lightly, and for as little noise as the traitors made in rising, he was awakened by it, and starting up, drew his sword, and went to meet them. At the same moment he pushed his foster-brother with his foot, to awaken him, and he got on his feet; but ere he got his eyes cleared to see what was about to happen, one of the ruffians that were advancing to slay the king, killed him with a stroke of his sword. The king was now alone, one man against three, and in the greatest danger of his life; but his amazing strength, and the good armour which he wore, freed him once more from this great peril, and he killed the three men, one after another.

He then left the cottage, very sorrowful for the death of his faithful foster-brother, and took his direction towards the place where he had appointed his men to assemble after their dispersion. It was now near night, and the place of meeting being a farm-house, he went boldly into it, where he found the mistress, an old true-hearted Scotswoman, sitting alone. Upon seeing a stranger enter, she asked him who and what he was. The king answered that he was a traveller, who was journeying through the country.

"All travellers," answered the good woman, "are welcome here, for the sake of one."

"And who is that one," said the king, "for whose sake you make all travellers welcome?"

"It is our rightful king, Robert the Bruce," answered the mistress, "who is the lawful lord of this country; and although he is now pursued and hunted after with hounds and horns, I hope to live to see him king over all Scotland."

"Since you love him so well, dame," said the king, "know that you see him before you. I am Robert the Bruce."

"You!" said the good woman, in great surprise; "and wherefore are you thus alone?—where are all your men?"

"I have none with me at this moment," answered Bruce, "and therefore I must travel alone."

"But that shall not be," said the brave old dame, "for I have two stout sons, gallant and trusty men, who shall be your servants for life and death."

So she brought her two sons, and though she well knew the dangers to which she exposed them, she made them swear fidelity to the king; and they afterwards became high officers in his service.

THE BLACK DOUGLAS

I. *The Douglas Larder*

EDWARD THE SECOND was neither so brave nor so wise
as his father: on the contrary, he was a weak prince, fond
of idle amusements, and worthless favourites. It was
lucky for Scotland that such was his disposition. He
marched a little way into Scotland with the large army
which Edward the First had collected, but retired without
fighting; which gave great encouragement to Bruce's party.

Several of the Scottish nobility now took arms in
different parts of the country, declared for King Robert,
and fought against the English troops and garrisons,
The most distinguished of these was the good Lord James
of Douglas, whom we have often mentioned before.
Some of his most memorable exploits respected his own
castle of Douglas, in which, being an important fortress,
and strongly situated, the English had placed a large
garrison. James of Douglas saw, with great displeasure,
his castle filled with English soldiers, and stored with
great quantities of corn, and cattle, and wine, and ale,
and other supplies which they were preparing, to enable
them to assist the English with provisions. So he
resolved, if possible, to be revenged upon the captain
of the garrison and his soldiers.

For this purpose, Douglas went in disguise to the house
of one of his old servants, called Thomas Dickson, a
strong, faithful, and bold man, and laid a scheme for
taking the castle. A holiday was approaching, called
Palm Sunday. Upon this day it was common, in the
Roman Catholic times, that the people went to church
in procession, with green boughs in their hands. Just
as the English soldiers, who had marched down from the

castle, got into church, one of Lord James's followers raised the cry of *Douglas ! Douglas !* which was the shout with which that family always began battle. Thomas Dickson and some friends whom he had collected instantly drew their swords and killed the first Englishman whom they met. But as the signal had been given too soon, Dickson was borne down and slain. Douglas and his men presently after forced their way into the church. The English soldiers attempted to defend themselves; but, being taken by surprise and unprepared, they were, for the greater part, killed or made prisoners, and that so suddenly, and with so little noise, that their companions in the castle never heard of it. So that when Douglas and his men approached the castle gate, they found it open, and that part of the garrison which were left at home, busied cooking provisions for those that were at church. So Lord James got possession of his castle without difficulty, and he and his men ate up all the good dinner which the English had made ready. But Douglas dared not stay there, lest the English should come in great force and besiege him; and therefore he resolved to destroy all the provisions which the English had stored up in the castle, and to render the place unavailing to them.

It must be owned he executed this purpose in a very cruel and shocking manner, for he was much enraged at the death of Thomas Dickson. He caused all the barrels containing flour, meal, wheat, and malt, to be knocked in pieces, and their contents mixed on the floor; then he staved the great hogsheads of wine and ale, and mixed the liquor with the stores; and, last of all, he killed his prisoners, and flung the dead bodies among this disgusting heap, which his men called, in derision of the English, the Douglas Larder. Then he flung dead horses into the

well to destroy it—after which he set fire to the castle;
and finally marched away, and took refuge with his
followers in the hills and forests. "He loved better," he
said, "to hear the lark sing than the mouse squeak."
That is, he loved better to keep in the open field with his
men, than to shut himself and them up in castles.

When Clifford, the English general, heard what had
happened, he came to Douglas Castle with a great body
of men, and rebuilt all the defences which Lord James
had destroyed, and cleared out the well, and put a good
soldier, named Thirlwall, to command the garrison, and
desired him to be on his guard, for he suspected that
Lord James would again attack him. And, indeed,
Douglas, who did not like to see the English in his father's
castle, was resolved to take the first opportunity of
destroying this garrison, as he had done the former. For
this purpose he again had recourse to stratagem. He laid
a part of his followers in ambush in the wood, and
sent fourteen men, disguised like countrymen, driving
cattle past the gates of the castle. As soon as Thirlwall
saw this, he swore that he would plunder the Scots
drovers of their cattle, and came out with a considerable
part of his garrison for that purpose. He had followed the
cattle past the place where Douglas was lying concealed,
when all of a sudden the Scotsmen threw off their carriers'
cloaks, and appearing in armour, cried the cry of Douglas,
and, turning back suddenly, ran to meet the pursuers;
and before Thirlwall could make any defence, he heard
the same war-cry behind him, and saw Douglas coming
up with those Scots who had been lying in ambush.
Thirlwall himself was killed, fighting bravely in the middle
of his enemies, and only a very few of his men found their
way back to the castle.

When Lord James had thus slain two English com-

manders or governors of his castle, and was known to
have made a vow that he would be revenged on any one
who should dare to take possession of his father's house,
men became afraid; and the fortress was called, both in
England and Scotland, the Perilous Castle of Douglas,
because it proved so dangerous to any Englishman who
was stationed there. . . .

At the time we speak of, there was a young lady in
England whom many knights and noblemen asked in
marriage, because she was extremely wealthy, and very
beautiful. Once upon a holiday she made a great feast,
to which she asked all her lovers, and numerous other
gallant knights; and after the feast she arose and told
them that she was much obliged to them for their good
opinion of her, but as she desired to have for her husband
a man of the most incontestable bravery, she had formed
her resolution not to marry any one save one who should
show his courage by defending the Perilous Castle of
Douglas against the Scots for a year and a day. Now
this made some silence among the gentlemen present; for
although the lady was rich and beautiful, yet there was
great danger in placing themselves within the reach of
the Good Lord James of Douglas. At last a brave young
knight started up and said, that for the love of that lady
he was willing to keep the Perilous Castle for a year
and a day, if the king pleased to give him leave. The
king of England was satisfied, and well pleased to get
a brave man to hold a place so dangerous. Sir John
Wilton was the name of this gallant knight. He kept the
castle very safely for some time; but Douglas at last, by
a stratagem, induced him to venture out with a part of
the garrison, and then set upon them and slew them.
Wilton himself was killed, and a letter from the lady was
found in his pocket. Douglas was sorry for his unhappy

end, and did not put to death any of the prisoners as he had formerly done, but dismissed them in safety to the next English garrison.

Other great lords, besides Douglas, were now exerting themselves to attack and destroy the English. Amongst those was Sir Thomas Randolph, whose mother was a sister of King Robert. . . . There was a sort of rivalry between Douglas and him, which should do the boldest and most hazardous actions. I will just mention one or two circumstances, which will show you what awful dangers were to be encountered by these brave men in order to free Scotland from its enemies and invaders.

II. *How Sir Thomas Randolph took Edinburgh Castle*

While Robert Bruce was gradually getting possession of the country, and driving out the English, Edinburgh, the principal town of Scotland, remained, with its strong castle, in possession of the invaders. Sir Thomas Randolph was extremely desirous to gain this important place; but the castle is situated on a very steep and lofty rock, so that it is difficult or almost impossible even to get up to the foot of the walls, much more to climb over them.

So while Randolph was considering what was to be done, there came to him a Scottish gentleman named Francis, who had joined Bruce's standard, and asked to speak with him in private. He then told Randolph that in his youth he had lived in the castle of Edinburgh and that his father had then been keeper of the fortress. It happened at that time that Francis was much in love with a lady who lived in a part of the town beneath the castle, which is called the Grassmarket. Now, as he could not get out of the castle by day to see his mistress, he had practised a way of clambering by night down the castle rock on the south side, and returning at his pleasure;

when he came to the foot of the wall, he made use of a ladder to get over it, as it was not very high at that point, those who built it having trusted to the steepness of the crag; and, for the same reason, no watch was placed there. Francis had gone and come so frequently in this dangerous manner that, though it was now long ago, he told Randolph he knew the road so well, that he would undertake to guide a small party of men by night to the bottom of the wall; and as they might bring ladders with them, there would be no difficulty in scaling it. The great risk was, that of their being discovered by the watchmen while in the act of ascending the cliff, in which case every man of them must have perished.

Nevertheless, Randolph did not hesitate to attempt the adventure. He took with him only thirty men (you may be sure they were chosen for activity and courage), and came one dark night to the foot of the rock, which they began to ascend under the guidance of Francis, who went before them upon his hands and feet, up one cliff, down another, and round another, where there was scarce room to support themselves. All the while, these thirty men were obliged to follow in a line, one after the other, by a path that was fitter for a cat than a man. The noise of a stone falling, or a word spoken from one to another, would have alarmed the watchmen. They were obliged, therefore, to move with the greatest precaution. When they were far up the crag, and near the foundation of the wall, they heard the guards going their rounds, to see that all was safe in and about the castle. Randolph and his party had nothing for it but to lie close and quiet, each man under the crag, as he happened to be placed, and trust that the guards would pass by without noticing them. And while they were waiting in breathless alarm, they got a new cause of fright. One of the soldiers of the castle, willing to startle his comrades, suddenly threw a stone from the wall, and cried out, "Aha, I see you well!" The stone came thundering down over the heads of Randolph and his men, who naturally thought themselves discovered. If they had stirred, or made the slightest noise, they would have been entirely destroyed; for the soldiers above might have killed every man of them merely by rolling down stones. But being courageous and chosen men, they remained quiet, and the English soldiers, who thought their comrade was merely playing them a trick (as, indeed, he had no other meaning in what he did and said), passed on, without further examination.

Then Randolph and his men got up, and came in haste to the foot of the wall, which was not above twice a man's height in that place. They planted the ladders they had brought, and Francis mounted first to show them the way; Sir Andrew Grey, a brave knight, followed him, and Randolph himself was the third man who got over. Then the rest followed. When once they were within the walls, there was not so much to do, for the garrison were asleep and unarmed, excepting the watch, who were speedily destroyed. Thus was Edinburgh Castle taken in March 1312-13.

III. *A Load of Hay*

It was not, however, only by the exertions of great and powerful barons, like Randolph and Douglas, that the freedom of Scotland was to be accomplished. The stout yeomanry, and the bold peasantry of the land, who were as desirous to enjoy their cottages in honourable independence as the nobles were to reclaim their castles and estates from the English, contributed their full share in the efforts which were made to deliver their country from the invaders. I will give you one instance among many.

There was a strong castle near Linlithgow, or Lithgow, as the word is more generally pronounced, where an English governor, with a powerful garrison, lay in readiness to support the English cause, and used to exercise much severity upon the Scots in the neighbourhood. There lived, at no great distance from the stronghold, a farmer, a bold and stout man, whose name was Binnock, or as it is now pronounced, Binning. This man saw with great joy the progress which the Scots were making in recovering their country from the English, and resolved to do something to help his countrymen, by getting possession, if it were possible, of the castle of Lithgow. But the place was very strong, situated by the side of a lake, defended not only by gates, which were usually kept shut against strangers, but also by a portcullis. A portcullis is a sort of door formed of crossbars of iron, like a grate. It has not hinges like a door, but is drawn up by pulleys, and let down when any danger approaches. It may be let go in a moment; and then falls down into the doorway; and as it has great iron spikes at the bottom, it crushes all that it lights upon; thus in case of a sudden alarm, a portcullis may be let suddenly fall to defend the entrance, when it is not possible to shut the gates. Binnock knew this very well, but he resolved to be provided against this risk also when he attempted to surprise the castle. So he spoke with some bold courageous countrymen, and engaged them in his enterprise, which he accomplished thus:

Binnock had been accustomed to supply the garrison of Linlithgow with hay, and he had been ordered by the English governor to furnish some cart-loads, of which they were in want. He promised to bring it accordingly; but the night before he drove the hay to the castle, he stationed a party of his friends, as well armed as possible, near the entrance, where they could not be seen by the garrison, and gave them directions that they should come to his assistance as soon as they should hear him cry a signal, which was to be, "Call all, call all!" Then he loaded a great waggon with hay. But in the waggon he placed eight strong men, well armed, lying flat on their breasts, and covered over with hay, so that they could not be seen. He himself walked carelessly beside the waggon; and he chose the stoutest and bravest of his servants to be the driver, who carried at his belt a strong axe or hatchet. In this way Binnock approached the castle early in the morning; and the watchman, who only saw two men, Binnock being one of them, with a cart of hay, which they expected, opened the gates, and raised up the portcullis, to permit them to enter the castle. But as soon as the cart had gotten under the gateway, Binnock made a sign to his servant, who with his axe suddenly cut asunder the *soam*, that is, the yoke which fastens the horses to the cart, and the horses finding themselves free, naturally started forward, the cart remaining behind under the arch of the gate. At the same moment, Binnock cried as loud as he could, "Call all, call all!" and drawing the sword which he had under his country habit, he killed the porter. The armed men then jumped up from under the hay where they lay concealed, and rushed on the English guard. The Englishmen tried to shut the gates, but they could not because the cart of hay remained in the gateway, and prevented the folding doors from being closed. The portcullis was also let fall, but the grating was caught on the cart, and so could not drop to the ground. The men who were in ambush near the gate, hearing the cry, "Call all, call all!" ran to assist those who had leaped out from amongst the hay; the castle was taken, and all the Englishmen killed or

c

made prisoners. King Robert rewarded Binnock by bestowing on him an estate, which his posterity long afterwards enjoyed.

IV. *Black Cattle*

Perhaps you may be tired, my dear child, of such stories; yet I will tell you how the great and important castle of Roxburgh was taken from the English, and then we will pass to other subjects.

You must know Roxburgh was then a very large castle, situated near where two fine rivers, the Tweed and the Teviot, join each other. Being within five or six miles of England, the English were extremely desirous of retaining it, and the Scots equally eager to obtain possession of it. I will tell you how it was taken.

It was upon the night of what is called Shrovetide, a holiday which Roman Catholics paid great respect to, and solemnised with much gaiety and feasting. Most of the garrison of Roxburgh Castle were drinking and carousing, but still they had set watches on the battlements of the castle, in case of any sudden attack; for, as the Scots had succeeded in so many enterprises of the kind, and as Douglas was known to be in the neighbourhood, they conceived themselves obliged to keep a very strict guard.

An Englishwoman, the wife of one of the officers, was sitting on the battlements with her child in her arms; and looking out on the fields below, she saw some black objects, like a herd of cattle, straggling near the foot of the wall, and approaching the ditch or moat of the castle. She pointed them out to the sentinel, and asked him what they were. "Pooh, pooh," said the soldier, "it is farmer such a one's cattle" (naming a man whose farm lay near to the castle); "the good man is keeping a jolly Shrovetide, and has forgot to shut up his bullocks in their yard; but if the Douglas come across them before morning, he is likely to rue his negligence." Now these creeping objects which they saw from the castle wall were no real cattle, but Douglas himself and his soldiers, who had put black cloaks above their armour, and were creeping about on hands and feet, in order, without being observed, to get so near to the foot of the castle wall as to be able to set ladders to it. The poor woman, who knew nothing of this, sat quietly on the wall, and began to sing to her child. You must know that the name of Douglas had become so terrible to the English that the women used to frighten their children with it, and say to them, when they behaved ill, that they "would make the Black Douglas take them." And this soldier's wife was singing to her child:

> Hush ye, hush ye, little pet ye,
> Hush ye, hush ye, do not fret ye,
> The Black Douglas shall not get ye.

"You are not so sure of that," said a voice close beside her. She felt at the same time a heavy hand, with an iron glove, laid on her shoulder, and when she looked round, she saw the very Black Douglas she had been singing about, standing close beside her, a tall, swarthy, strong man. At the same time, another Scotsman was seen ascending the walls, near to the sentinel. The soldier gave the alarm, and rushed at the Scotsman, whose name was Simon Ledehouse, with his lance; but Simon parried the stroke, and closing with the sentinel, struck him a deadly blow with his dagger. The rest of the Scots followed up to assist Douglas and Ledehouse, and the castle was taken. Many of the soldiers were put to death, but Douglas protected the woman and the child. I daresay she made no more songs about the Black Douglas.

THE PERCY AND THE DOUGLAS

It was from prudence, not from want of courage, that the Scots avoided great battles with the English. They readily engaged in smaller actions, when they fought with the utmost valour on both sides, till, as an old historian expresses it, sword and lance could endure no longer, and then they would part from each other, saying, "Good day; and thanks for the sport you have shown." A very remarkable instance of such a desperate battle occurred in the year 1388.

The Scottish nobles had determined upon an invasion of England on a large scale, and had assembled a great army for that purpose; but learning that the people of Northumberland were raising an army on the eastern frontier, they resolved to limit their incursion to that which might be achieved by the Earl of Douglas, with a chosen band of four or five thousand men. With this force he penetrated into the mountainous frontier of England, where an assault was least expected, and issuing forth near Newcastle, fell upon the flat and rich country around, slaying, plundering, burning, and loading his army with spoil.

Percy, Earl of Northumberland, an English noble of great power, and with whom the Douglas had frequently had encounters, sent his two sons, Sir Henry and Sir Ralph Percy, to stop the progress of this invasion. Both were gallant knights; but the first, who, from his impetuosity, was called Hotspur, was one of the most

distinguished warriors in England, as Douglas was in
Scotland. The brothers threw themselves hastily into Newcastle, to defend that important town; and as Douglas,
in an insulting manner, drew up his followers before the
walls, they came out to skirmish with the Scots. Douglas
and Henry Percy encountered personally; and it so
chanced that Douglas in the struggle got possession of
Hotspur's spear, to the end of which was attached a
small ornament of silk, embroidered with pearls, on
which was represented a lion, the cognisance, as it is
called, of the Percies. Douglas shook this trophy aloft,
and declared that he would carry it into Scotland, and
plant it on his castle of Dalkeith.

"That," said Percy, "shalt thou never do. I will
regain my lance ere thou canst get back into Scotland."

"Then," said Douglas, "come to seek it, and thou
shalt find it before my tent."

The Scottish army, having completed the purpose of
their expedition, began their retreat up the vale of the
little river Reed, which afforded a tolerable road running
north - westward towards their own frontier. They en-
camped at Otterburn, about twenty miles from the
Scottish border, on 19th August, 1388.

In the middle of the night the alarm arose in the Scottish camp that the English host were coming upon them,
and the moonlight showed the approach of Sir Henry
Percy, with a body of men superior in number to that of
Douglas. He had already crossed the Reed water, and
was advancing towards the left flank of the Scottish
army. Douglas, not choosing to receive the assault in
that position, drew his men out of the camp, and with
a degree of military skill which could scarce have been
expected when his forces were of such an undisciplined
character, he altogether changed the position of the

army, and presented his troops with their front to the advancing English.

Hotspur, in the meantime, marched his squadrons through the deserted camp, where there were none left but a few servants and stragglers of the army. The interruptions which the English troops met with threw them a little into disorder, when the moon arising showed them the Scottish army, which they had supposed to be retreating, drawn up in complete order, and prepared to fight. The battle commenced with the greatest fury; for Percy and Douglas were the two most distinguished soldiers of their time, and each army trusted in the courage and talents of their commanders, whose names were shouted on either side. The Scots, who were outnumbered, were at length about to give way, when Douglas, their leader, caused his banner to advance, attended by his best men. He himself shouting his war-cry of "Douglas!" rushed forward, clearing his way with the blows of his battle-axe, and breaking into the very thickest of the enemy. He fell, at length, under three mortal wounds. Had his death been observed by the enemy, the event would probably have decided the battle against the Scots; but the English only knew that some brave man-at-arms had fallen. Meantime the other Scottish nobles pressed forward, and found their general dying among several of his faithful esquires and pages, who lay slain around. A stout priest, called William of North Berwick, the chaplain of Douglas, was protecting the body of his wounded patron with a long lance.

"How fares it, cousin?" said Sinclair, the first Scottish knight who came up to the expiring leader.

"Indifferently," answered Douglas; "but blessed be God, my ancestors have died in fields of battle, not on down-beds. I sink fast; but let them still cry my war-cry.

and conceal my death from my followers. There was a tradition in our family that a dead Douglas should win a field, and I trust it will be this day accomplished."

The nobles did as he had enjoined; they concealed the earl's body, and again rushed on to the battle, shouting "Douglas! Douglas!" louder than before. The English were weakened by the loss of the brave brothers, Henry and Ralph Percy, both of whom were made prisoners, fighting most gallantly, and almost no man of note amongst the English escaped death or captivity. Hence a Scottish poet has said of the name of Douglas:

> Hosts have been known at that dread sound to yield,
> And, Douglas dead, his name hath won the field.

Sir Henry Percy became the prisoner of Sir Hugh Montgomery, who obliged him for ransom to build a castle for him at Penoon in Ayrshire. The battle of Otterburn was disastrous to the leaders on both sides—Percy being made captive, and Douglas slain on the field. It has been the subject of many songs and poems, and the great historian Froissart says that, one other action only excepted, it was the best fought battle of that warlike time.

HALF-A-CROWN'S WORTH OF FIGHTING

It happened, fortunately perhaps for the Lowlands, that the wild Highlanders were as much addicted to quarrel with each other as with their Lowland neighbours. Two clans, or rather two leagues or confederacies, composed each of several separate clans, fell into such deadly feud with each other as filled the whole neighbourhood with slaughter and discord.

When this feud or quarrel could be no otherwise ended, it was resolved that the difference should be decided by a combat of thirty men of the Clan Chattan, against the same number of the Clan Kay; that the battle should take place on the North Inch of Perth, a beautiful and level meadow, in part surrounded by the river Tay; and that it should be fought in presence of the king and his nobles. Now there was a cruel policy in this arrangement; for it was to be supposed that all the best and leading men of each clan would desire to be among the thirty which were to fight for their honour, and it was no less to be expected that the battle would be very bloody and desperate. Thus, the probable event would be, that both clans, having lost very many of their best and bravest men, would be more easily managed in future. Such was probably the view of the king and his counsellors in permitting this desperate conflict, which, however, was much in the spirit of the times.

The parties on each side were drawn out, armed with sword and target, axe and dagger, and stood looking on each other with fierce and savage aspects, when, just as the signal for fight was expected, the commander of the Clan Chattan perceived that one of his men, whose heart had failed him, had deserted his standard. There was no time to seek another man from the clan, as his only resource, was obliged to offer a reward to any one who would fight in the room of the fugitive. Perhaps you think it might be difficult to get a man who, for a small hire, would undergo the perils of a battle which was likely to be so obstinate and deadly. But in that fighting age men valued their lives lightly. One Henry Wynd, a citizen of Perth, and a saddler by trade, a little bandy-legged man, but of great strength and activity, and well accustomed to use the broadsword, offered himself, for half a French crown, to serve on the part of the Clan Chattan in the battle of that day.

The signal was then given by sound of the royal trumpets, and of the great war-bagpipes of the Highlanders, and the two parties fell on each other with the utmost fury; their natural ferocity of temper being excited by feudal hatred against the hostile clan, zeal for the honour of their own, and a consciousness that they were fighting in presence of the king and nobles of Scotland. As they fought with the two-handed sword and axe, the wounds they inflicted on each other were of a ghastly size and character. Heads were cloven asunder, limbs were lopped from the trunk. The meadow was soon drenched with blood, and covered with dead and wounded men.

In the midst of the deadly conflict, the chieftain of the Clan Chattan observed that Henry Wynd, after he had slain one of the Clan Kay, drew aside, and did not seem willing to fight more.

"How is this," said he, "art thou afraid?"

* C

"Not I," answered Henry; "but I have done enough of work for half-a-crown."

"Forward and fight," said the Highland chief; "he that doth not grudge his day's work, I will not stint him in his wages."

Thus encouraged, Henry Wynd again plunged into the conflict, and, by his excellence as a swordsman, contributed a great deal to the victory, which at length fell to the Clan Chattan. Ten of the victors, with Henry Wynd, whom the Highlanders called the *Gow Chrom* (that is, the crooked or bandy-legged smith, for he was both a smith and a saddler, war-saddles being then made of steel), were left alive, but they were all wounded. Only one of the Clan Kay survived, and he was unhurt. But this single individual dared not oppose himself to eleven men, though all more or less injured, but, throwing himself into the Tay, swam to the other side, and went off to carry to the Highlands the news of his clan's defeat. It is said, he was so ill received by his kinsmen that he put himself to death.

Some part of the above story is matter of tradition, but the general fact is certain. Henry Wynd was rewarded to the Highland chieftain's best abilities; but it was remarked that, when the battle was over, he was not able to tell the name of the clan he had fought for, replying, when asked on which side he had been, that he was fighting for his own. Hence the proverb, "Every man for his own hand, as Henry Wynd fought."

A KING'S TRAGEDY

THUS James I. restored a considerable degree of tranquillity to the country, which he found in such a distracted state. He made wise laws for regulating the commerce of the nation, both at home and with other states, and strict regulations for the administration of justice betwixt those who had complaints against one another.

But his greatest labour, and that which he found most difficult to accomplish, was to diminish the power of the great nobles, who ruled like so many kings, each on his own territory and estate, and made war on the king, or upon one another, whenever it was their pleasure to do so. These disorders he endeavoured to check, and had several of these great persons brought to trial, and, upon their being found guilty, deprived them of their estates. The nobles complained that this was done out of spite against them, and that they were treated with hardship and injustice; and thus discontents were entertained against this good prince. Another cause of offence was, that to maintain justice, and support the authority of the throne, it was found necessary that some taxes for this purpose should be raised from the subjects; and the Scottish people being poor, and totally unaccustomed to pay any such contributions, they imputed this odious measure to the king's avarice. And thus, though King James was so well-intentioned a king, and certainly the ablest who had reigned in Scotland since the days of Robert Bruce, yet both the high and the low murmured against him, which encouraged some wicked men amongst the nobility to conspire his death.

The chief person in the plot was one Sir Robert Graham, uncle to the Earl of Stratherne. He was bold and ambitious, and highly offended with the king on account of an imprisonment which he had sustained by the royal command. He drew into the plot the Earl of Athole, an old man of little talent, by promising to make his son, Sir Robert Stewart, King of Scotland, in place of James. Others were engaged in the conspiracy from different motives. To many of their attendants they pretended they only wished to carry away a lady out of the court. To prepare his scheme, Graham retreated into the remote Highlands, and from thence sent a defiance, renouncing his allegiance to the king, and threatening to put his sovereign to death with his own hand. A price was set upon his head, payable to any one who should deliver him up to justice; but he lay concealed in the wild mountains to prosecute his revenge against James.

The Christmas preceding his murder was appointed by the king for holding a feast at Perth. In his way to that town he was met by a Highland woman, calling herself a prophetess. She stood by the side of the ferry by which he was about to travel to the north, and cried with a loud voice, "My lord the king, if you pass this water, you will never return again alive." The king was struck with this for a moment, because he had read in a book that a king should be slain that year in Scotland; for it often happens, that when a remarkable deed is in agitation, rumours of it get abroad, and are repeated under pretence of prophecies; but which are, in truth, only conjectures of that which seems likely to happen. There was a knight in the court, on whom the king had conferred the name of the King of Love, to whom the king said in jest, "There is a prophecy that a king shall be killed in Scotland this year; now, Sir Alexander, that must concern either you or me, since we two are the only kings in Scotland." Other circumstances occurred which might have prevented the good king's murder, but none of them were attended to. The king, while at Perth, took up his residence in an abbey of Black Friars, there being no castle or palace in the town convenient for his residence; and this made the execution of the conspiracy more easy, as his guards, and the officers of his household, were quartered among the citizens.

The day had been spent by the king in sport and feasting, and by the conspirators in preparing for their enterprise. They had destroyed the locks of the doors of the apartment, so that the keys could not be turned; and they had taken away the bars with which the gates were secured, and had provided planks by way of bridges, on which to cross the ditch which surrounded the monastery. At length, on the 20th February, 1437, all was prepared for carrying their treasonable purpose into execution, and Graham came from his hiding-place in the neighbouring mountains, with a party of nigh three hundred men, and entered the gardens of the convent.

The king was in his night-gown and slippers. He had passed the evening gaily with the nobles and ladies of his court, in reading romances, and in singing and music, or playing at chess and tables. The Earl of Athole, and his son Sir Robert Stewart, who expected to succeed James on the throne, were among the last courtiers who retired. At this time James remained standing before the fire, and conversing gaily with the queen and her ladies before he went to rest. The Highland woman before mentioned again demanded permission to speak with the king, but was refused, on account of the untimeliness of the hour. All now were ordered to withdraw.

At this moment there was a noise and clashing heard, as of men in armour, and the torches in the garden cast up great flashes of light against the windows. The king then recollected his deadly enemy, Sir Robert Graham, and guessed that he was coming to murder him. He called to the ladies who were left in the chamber to keep the door as well as they could, in order to give him time to escape. He first tried to get out at the windows, but they were fast barred, and defied his strength. By help of the tongs, which were in the chimney, he raised, however, a plank of the flooring of the apartment, and let himself down into a narrow vault beneath, used as a common sewer. This vault had formerly had an opening into the court of the convent, by which he might have made his escape. But all things turned against the unfortunate James; for, only three days before, he had caused the opening to be built up, because when he played at ball in the court-yard, the ball used to roll into the vault through that hole.

While the king was in this place of concealment, the conspirators were seeking him from chamber to chamber throughout the convent, and, at length, came to the room where the ladies were. The queen and her women endeavoured, as well as they might, to keep the door shut, and one of them, Catherine Douglas, boldly thrust her own arms across the door, instead of the bar, which had been taken away, as I told you. But the brave lady's arm was soon broken, and the traitors rushed into the room with swords and daggers drawn, hurting and throwing down such of the women as opposed them.

The poor queen stood half undressed, shrieking aloud; and one of the brutal assassins attacked, wounded, and would have slain her, had it not been for a son of Sir Robert Graham, who said to him, "What would you do to the queen? She is but a woman—Let us seek the king."

They accordingly commenced a minute search, but without any success; so they left the apartment, and sought elsewhere about the monastery. In the meanwhile the king turned impatient, and desired the ladies to bring sheets and draw him up out of the inconvenient lurking-place. In the attempt Elizabeth Douglas fell down beside the king, and at this unlucky moment the conspirators returned. One of them now recollected that there was such a vault, and that they had not searched it. And when they tore up the plank, and saw the king and the lady beneath in the vault, one of them called, with savage merriment to his followers, "Sirs, I have found the bride for whom we have sought and carolled all night." Then, first one and then another of the villains, brethren of the name of Hall, descended into the vault, with daggers drawn, to despatch the unfortunate king, who was standing there in his shirt, without weapons of any kind. But James, who was an active and strong man, threw them both down beneath his feet, and struggled to wrest the dagger from one or other of them, in which attempt his hands were severely cut and mangled. The murderers also were so vigorously handled, that the marks of the king's gripe were visible on their throats for weeks afterwards. Then Sir Robert Graham himself sprang down on the king, who finding no further defence possible, asked him for mercy, and for leisure to confess his sins to a priest. But Graham replied fiercely, "Thou never hadst mercy on those of thine own blood, nor on any one else, therefore thou shalt find no mercy here; and as for a confessor, thou shalt have none but this sword." So speaking he thrust the sword through the king's body. And yet it is said, that when he saw his prince lying bleeding under his feet, he was desirous to have left the enterprise unfinished; but the other conspirators called on Graham to kill the king, otherwise he should himself die by their hands; upon which Graham, with the two men who had descended into the vault before him, fell on the unhappy prince with their daggers, and slew him by many stabs. There were sixteen wounds in his breast alone.

THE LAST FIGHT OF A SCOTTISH SAILOR

James IV. had been extremely desirous to increase the strength of his kingdom by sea, and its commerce; and Scotland presenting a great extent of sea-coast, and numerous harbours, had at this time a considerable trade. The royal navy, besides one vessel called the *Great Michael*, supposed to be the largest in the world, and which, as an old author says, "cumbered all Scotland to get her fitted out for sea," consisted, it is said, of sixteen ships of war. The king paid particular attention to naval affairs, and seemed never more happy than when inspecting and exercising his little navy. It chanced that one John Barton, a Scottish mariner, had been captured by the Portuguese, as far back as the year 1476. As the King of Portugal refused to make any amends, James granted the family of Barton letters of reprisals, that is, a warrant empowering them to take all Portuguese vessels which should come in their way, until their loss was made up. There were three brothers, all daring men, but especially the eldest, whose name was Andrew Barton. He had two strong ships, the larger called the *Lion*, the lesser the *Jenny Pirwen*, with which it would appear he cruised in the British Channel, stopping not only Portuguese vessels, but also English ships bound for Portugal. Complaints being made to King Henry, he fitted out two vessels, which were filled with chosen men, and placed under the command of Lord Thomas Howard and Sir Edward Howard, both sons to the Earl of Surrey. They found Barton and his vessels cruising in the Downs, being guided to the place by the captain of a merchant vessel whom Barton had plundered on the preceding day.

On approaching the enemy, the noble brothers showed no ensign of war, but put up a willow wand on their masts, as being the emblem of a trading vessel. But when the Scotsman attempted to make them bring to, the English threw out their flags and pennons, and fired a broadside of their ordnance. Barton then knew that he was engaged with the King of England's ships of war. Far from being dismayed at this, he engaged boldly, and, distinguished by his rich dress and bright armour, appeared on deck with a whistle of gold about his neck, suspended by a chain of the same precious metal, and encouraged his men to fight valiantly.

The fight was very obstinate. If we may believe a ballad of the time, Barton's ship was furnished with a peculiar contrivance, suspending large weights, or beams, from his yard-arms, to be dropped down upon the enemy when they should come alongside. To make use of this contrivance, it was necessary that a person should ascend the mainmast, or in naval language, go aloft. As the English apprehended much mischief from the consequences of this manœuvre, Howard had stationed a Yorkshire gentleman, named Hustler, the best archer in the ship, with strict injunctions to shoot everyone who should attempt to go aloft to let fall the beams of Barton's vessel. Two men were successively killed in the attempt, and Andrew Barton himself, confiding in the strong armour which he wore, began to ascend the mast. Lord Thomas Howard called out to the archer to shoot true, on peril of his life. "Were I to die for it," said Hustler, "I have but two arrows left." The first which he shot bounded from Barton's armour without hurting him; but as the Scottish mariner raised his arm to climb higher, the archer took aim where the armour afforded him no protection, and wounded him mortally through the arm-pit.

Barton descended from the mast. "Fight on," he said, "my brave hearts; I am a little wounded, but not slain. I will but rest a while, and then rise and fight again; meantime, stand fast by Saint Andrew's Cross," meaning the Scottish flag, or ensign. He encouraged his men with his whistle while the breath of life remained. At length the whistle was heard no longer, and the Howards, boarding the Scottish vessel, found that her daring captain was dead. They carried the *Lion* into the Thames, and it is remarkable that Barton's ship became the second man-of-war in the English navy. When the kings wanted to equip a fleet, they hired or pressed into their service merchant vessels, and put soldiers on board of them. The ship called the *Great Henry* was the first built especially for war, by the king, as his own property,—this captured vessel was the second.

FLODDEN FIELD

THE Scottish army had fixed their camp upon a hill
called Flodden, which rises to close in, as it were, the
extensive flat called Millfield Plain. This eminence slopes
steeply towards the plain, and there is an extended
piece of level ground on the top, where the Scots might
have drawn up their army, and awaited at great advantage the attack of the English. Surrey liked the idea of
venturing an assault on that position so ill, that he
resolved to try whether he could not prevail on the king
to abandon it. He sent a herald to invite James to come
down from the height, and join battle in the open plain
of Millfield below—reminded him of the readiness with
which he had accepted his former challenge—and hinted,
that it was the opinion of the English chivalry assembled
for battle, that any delay of the encounter would sound
to the king's dishonour.

We have seen that James was sufficiently rash and
imprudent, but his impetuosity did not reach to the
pitch Surrey perhaps expected. He refused to receive
the messenger into his presence, and returned for answer,
that it was not such a message as it became an earl to
send to a king.

Surrey, therefore, distressed for provisions, was obliged
to resort to another mode of bringing the Scots to action.
He moved northward, sweeping round the hill of Flodden,
keeping out of the reach of the Scottish artillery, until,
crossing the Till near Twisell Castle, he placed himself,
with his whole army, betwixt James and his own kingdom. The king suffered him to make this flank movement

without interruption, though it must have afforded repeated and advantageous opportunities for attack. But when he saw the English army interposed betwixt him and his dominions, he became alarmed lest he should be cut off from Scotland. In this apprehension he was confirmed by one Giles Musgrave, an Englishman, whose counsel he used upon the occasion, and who assured him, that if he did not descend and fight with the English army, the Earl of Surrey would enter Scotland, and lay waste the whole country. Stimulated by this apprehension, the king resolved to give signal for the fatal battle.

With this view the Scots set fire to their huts, and the other refuse and litter of their camp. The smoke spread along the side of the hill, and under its cover the army of King James descended the eminence, which is much less steep on the northern than the southern side, while the English advanced to meet them, both concealed from each other by the clouds of smoke.

The Scots descended in four strong columns, all marching parallel to each other, having a reserve of the Lothian men, commanded by Earl Bothwell. The English were also divided into four bodies, with a reserve of cavalry led by Dacre.

The battle commenced at the hour of four in the afternoon. The first which encountered was the left wing of the Scots, commanded by the Earl of Huntly and Lord Home, which overpowered and threw into disorder the right wing of the English, under Sir Edmund Howard. Sir Edmund was beaten down, his standard taken, and he himself in danger of instant death, when he was relieved by the Bastard Heron, who came up at the head of a band of determined outlaws like himself, and extricated Howard. It is alleged against Lord Home by many Scottish writers, that he ought to have improved his advantage, by hastening to the support of the next division of the Scottish army. It is even pretended, that he replied to those who urged him to go to the assistance of the king, that "the man did well that day who stood and saved himself." But this seems invented, partly to criminate Home, partly to account for the loss of the battle in some other way than by the superiority of the English. In reality, the English cavalry, under Dacre, which acted as a reserve, appear to have kept the victors in check; while Thomas Howard, the lord high admiral who commanded the second division of the English, bore down, and routed the Scottish division commanded by Crawford and Montrose, who were both slain. Thus matters went on the Scottish left.

Upon the extreme right of James's army, a division of Highlanders, consisting of the clans of MacKenzie, MacLean, and others, commanded by the Earls of Lennox and Argyle, were so insufferably annoyed by the volleys of the English arrows, that they broke their ranks, and, in despite of the cries, entreaties, and signals of De la Motte, the French ambassador, who endeavoured to stop them, rushed tumultuously down hill, and being attacked at once in flank and rear by Sir Edward Stanley with the men of Cheshire and Lancashire, were routed with great slaughter.

The only Scottish division which remains to be mentioned was commanded by James in person, and consisted of the choicest of his nobles and gentry, whose armour was so good that the arrows made but slight impression upon them. They were all on foot—the king himself had parted with his horse. They engaged the Earl of Surrey, who opposed to them the division which he personally commanded. The Scots attacked with the greatest fury, and, for a time, had the better. Surrey's squadrons were disordered, his standard in great danger, Bothwell and the Scottish reserve were advancing, and the English seemed in some risk of losing the battle. But Stanley, who had defeated the Highlanders, came up on one flank of the king's division; the admiral, who had conquered Crawford and Montrose, assailed them on the other. The Scots showed the most undaunted courage. Uniting themselves with the reserve under Bothwell, they formed into a circle, with their spears extended on every side, and fought obstinately. Bows being now useless, the English advanced on all sides with their bills, a huge weapon which made ghastly wounds. But they could not force the Scots either to break or retire, although the carnage among them was dreadful. James himself died amid his warlike peers and loyal gentry. He was twice wounded with arrows, and at length despatched with a bill. Night fell without the battle being absolutely decided, for the Scottish centre kept their ground, and Home and Dacre held each other at bay. But during the night, the remainder of the Scottish army drew off in silent despair from the bloody field, on which they left their king, and the flower of his nobility.

This great and decisive victory was gained by the Earl of Surrey on 9th September, 1513. The victors had about five thousand men slain, the Scots twice that number at least. But the loss lay not so much in the number of the slain, as in their rank and quality. The English lost very few men of distinction. The Scots left on the field the king, two bishops, two mitred abbots, twelve earls, thirteen lords, and five eldest sons of peers. The number of gentlemen slain was beyond calculation; there is scarcely a family of name in Scottish history who did not lose a relative there.

THE GOODMAN OF BALLENGIECH

JAMES V. had a custom of going about the country disguised as a private person, in order that he might hear
complaints which might not otherwise reach his ears,
and perhaps, that he might enjoy amusements which he
could not have partaken of in his avowed royal character.

When James V. travelled in disguise, he used a name
which was known only to some of his principal nobility
and attendants. He was called the Goodman (the tenant,
that is) of Ballengiech. Ballengiech is a steep pass which
leads down behind the castle of Stirling. Once upon a
time, when the court was feasting in Stirling, the king
sent for some venison from the neighbouring hills. The
deer were killed, and put on horses' backs to be trans-
ported to Stirling. Unluckily they had to pass the castle
gates of Arnpryor, belonging to a chief of the Buchanans,
who chanced to have a considerable number of guests
with him. It was late, and the company were rather short
of victuals, though they had more than enough of liquor.
The chief, seeing so much fat venison passing his very
door, seized on it, and to the expostulations of the keepers,
who told him it belonged to King James, he answered
insolently, that if James was king in Scotland, he,
Buchanan, was king in Kippen; being the name of the
district in which the castle of Arnpryor lay. On hearing
what had happened, the king got on horseback, and rode
instantly from Stirling to Buchanan's house, where he
found a strong fierce-looking Highlander, with an axe
on his shoulder, standing sentinel at the door. This grim

warder refused the king admittance, saying that the laird of Arnpryor was at dinner, and would not be disturbed. "Yet go up to the company, my good friend," said the king, "and tell him that the Goodman of Ballengiech is come to feast with the King of Kippen." The porter went grumbling into the house, and told his master that there was a fellow with a red beard at the gate, who called himself the Goodman of Ballengiech, who said he was come to dine with the King of Kippen. As soon as Buchanan heard these words, he knew that the king was come in person, and hastened down to kneel at James's feet, and to ask forgiveness for his insolent behaviour. But the king, who only meant to give him a fright, forgave him freely, and, going into the castle, feasted on his own venison which Buchanan had intercepted. Buchanan of Arnpryor was ever afterwards called the King of Kippen.

Upon another occasion, King James, being alone and in disguise, fell into a quarrel with some gypsies, or other vagrants, and was assaulted by four or five of them. This chanced to be very near the bridge of Cramond; so the king got on the bridge, which, as it was high and narrow, enabled him to defend himself with his sword against the number of persons by whom he was attacked. There was a poor man thrashing corn in a barn near by, who came out on hearing the noise of the scuffle, and seeing one man defending himself against numbers, gallantly took the king's part with his flail, to such good purpose that the gypsies were obliged to fly. The husbandman then took the king into the barn, brought him a towel, and water to wash the blood from his face and hands, and finally walked with him a little way towards Edinburgh, in case he should be again attacked. On the way, the king asked his companion

what and who he was. The labourer answered, that his
name was John Howieson, and that he was a bondsman
on the farm of Braehead, near Cramond, which belonged
to the King of Scotland. James then asked the poor
man if there was any wish in the world which he would
particularly desire should be gratified; and honest John
confessed he should think himself the happiest man in
Scotland were he but proprietor of the farm on which
he wrought as a labourer. He then asked the king, in
turn, who *he* was; and James replied as usual, that he
was the Goodman of Ballengiech, a poor man who had
a small appointment about the palace; but he added,
that if John Howieson would come to see him on the
next Sunday, he would endeavour to repay his manful
assistance, and, at least, give him the pleasure of seeing
the royal apartments.

John put on his best clothes, as you may suppose,
and appearing at a postern gate of the palace, inquired
for the Goodman of Ballengiech. The king had given
orders that he should be admitted; and John found his
friend, the goodman, in the same disguise which he had
formerly worn. The king, still preserving the character
of an inferior officer of the household, conducted John
Howieson from one apartment of the palace to another,
and was amused with his wonder and his remarks. At
length James asked his visitor if he should like to see
the king; to which John replied, nothing would delight
him so much, if he could do so without giving offence.
The Goodman of Ballengiech, of course, undertook that
the king would not be angry. "But," said John, "how
am I to know his Grace from the nobles who will be all
about him?"—"Easily," replied his companion; "all
the others will be uncovered—the king alone will wear
his hat or bonnet."

So speaking, King James introduced the countryman into a great hall, which was filled by the nobility and officers of the crown. John was a little frightened, and drew close to his attendant; but was still unable to distinguish the king. "I told you that you should know him by his wearing his hat," said the conductor. "Then," said John, after he had again looked round the room, "it must be either you or me, for all but us two are bare-headed."

The king laughed at John's fancy; and that the good yeoman might have occasion for mirth also, he made him a present of the farm of Braehead, which he had wished so much to possess, on condition that John Howieson, or his successors, should be ready to present a ewer and basin for the king to wash his hands, when his Majesty should come to Holyrood Palace, or should pass the bridge of Cramond. Accordingly, in the year 1822, when George IV. came to Scotland, the descendant of John Howieson of Braehead, who still possesses the estate which was given to his ancestor, appeared at a solemn festival, and offered his Majesty water from a silver ewer, that he might perform the service by which he held his lands.

THE RESCUE OF KINMONT WILLIE

THE English and Scottish wardens, or their deputies, had held a day of truce for settling Border disputes, and, having parted friends, both, with their followers, were returning home. At every such meeting it was the general rule on the Borders that there should be an absolute truce for twenty-four hours, and that all men who attended the warden on either side to the field should have permission to ride home again undisturbed.

Now, there had come to the meeting, with other Border men, a notorious depredator, called William Armstrong, but more commonly known by the name of Kinmont Willie. This man was riding home on the north or Scottish side of the Liddell, where that stream divides England and Scotland, when some of the English, who had enmity against him, or had suffered by his incursions, were unable to resist the temptation to attack him. They accordingly dashed across the river, pursued Kinmont Willie more than a mile within Scotland, made him prisoner, and brought him to Carlisle Castle.

As the man talked boldly and resolutely about the breach of truce in his person, and demanded peremptorily to be set at liberty, Lord Scrope told him scoffingly, that before he left the castle he should bid him "Farewell," meaning, that he should not go without his leave. The prisoner boldly answered, "That he would not go without bidding him good-night."

The Lord of Buccleuch, who was Warden, or Keeper, of Liddesdale, demanded the restoration of Kinmont

Willie to liberty, and complained of his being taken and imprisoned as a breach of the Border laws, and an insult done to himself. Lord Scrope refused, or at least evaded, giving up his prisoner. Buccleuch then sent him a challenge, which Lord Scrope declined to accept on the ground of his employment in the public service. The Scottish chief, therefore, resolved to redress by force the insult which his country as well as himself had sustained on the occasion. He collected about three hundred of his best men, and made a night march to Carlisle Castle. A small party of chosen men dismounted, while the rest remained on horseback, to repel any attack from the town. The night being misty and rainy, the party to whom that duty was committed approached the foot of the walls, and tried to scale them by means of ladders which they had brought with them for the purpose. But the ladders were found too short. They then, with mining instruments which they had provided, burst open a postern, or wicket-door, and entered the castle. Their chief had given them strict orders to do no harm save to those who opposed them, so that the few guards, whom the alarm brought together, were driven back without much injury. Being masters of the castle, the trumpets of the Scottish Warden were then blown, to the no small terror of the inhabitants of Carlisle, surprised out of their quiet sleep by the sounds of invasion at so early an hour. The bells of the castle rang out; those of the cathedral and moot-hall answered; drums beat to arms; and beacons were lighted, to alarm the warlike country around.

In the meanwhile, the Scottish party had done the errand they came for. They had freed Kinmont Willie from his dungeon. The first thing Armstrong did was to shout a good-night to Lord Scrope, asking him, at the same time, if he had any news for Scotland. The Borderers strictly obeyed the commands of their chief, in forbearing to take any booty. They returned from the castle, bringing with them their rescued countryman, and a gentleman named Spenser, an attendant on the constable of the castle. Buccleuch dismissed him, with his commendations to Salkeld the constable, whom he esteemed, he said, a better gentleman than Lord Scrope, bidding him say it was the Warden of Liddesdale who had done the exploit, and praying the constable, if he desired the name of a man of honour, to issue forth and seek a revenge. Buccleuch then ordered the retreat, which he performed with great leisure, and re-entered Scotland at sunrise in honour and safety. "There had never been a more gallant deed of vassalage done in Scotland," says an old historian, "no, not in Wallace's days."

A BORDER MARRIAGE

A YOUNG gentleman, of a distinguished family belonging to one of these Border tribes, or clans, made, either from the desire of plunder, or from revenge, a raid, or incursion, upon the lands of Sir Gideon Murray of Elibank, afterwards deputy treasurer of Scotland, and a great favourite of James VI. The Laird of Elibank, having got his people under arms, engaged the invaders, and, encountering them when they were encumbered with spoil, defeated them, and made the leader of the band prisoner. He was brought to the castle of his conqueror, when the lady inquired of her victorious husband, what he intended to do with his captive?—"I design," said the fierce baron, "to hang him instantly, dame, as a man taken red-hand in the act of robbery and violence." —"That is not like your wisdom, Sir Gideon," answered his more considerate lady. "If you put to death this young gentleman, you will enter into deadly feud with his numerous and powerful clan. You must therefore do a wiser thing, and, instead of hanging him, we will cause him to marry our youngest daughter, Meg with the meikle mouth, without any tocher" (that is, without any portion). The laird joyfully consented; for this Meg with the large mouth was so ugly, that there was very little chance of her getting a husband in any other circumstances; and in fact, when the alternative of such a marriage, or death by the gallows, was proposed to the poor prisoner, he was for some time disposed to choose the latter; nor was it without difficulty that he could be persuaded to save his life at the expense of marrying Meg Murray. He did so at last, however; and it is said that Meg, thus forced upon him, made an excellent and affectionate wife; but the unusual size of mouth was supposed to remain discernible in their descendants for several generations.

THE WESTERN ISLES

THE principal possessors of the Hebrides were originally of the name of MacDonald, the whole being under the government of a succession of chiefs, who bore the name of Donald of the Isles, and were possessed of authority almost independent of the Kings of Scotland. But this great family becoming divided into two or three branches, other chiefs settled in some of the islands, and disputed the property of the original proprietors. Thus, the MacLeods, a powerful and numerous clan, who had extensive estates on the mainland, made themselves masters, at a very early period, of a great part of the large island of Skye, seized upon much of the Long Island, as the Isles of Lewis and Harris are called, and fought fiercely with the MacDonalds, and other tribes of the islands. The following is an example of the mode in which these feuds were conducted.

About the end of the sixteenth century a boat, manned by one or two of the MacLeods, landed in Eigg, a small island peopled by the MacDonalds. They were at first hospitably received, but having been guilty of some incivility to the young women on the island, it was so much resented by the inhabitants, that they tied the MacLeods hand and foot, and putting them on board of their own boat, towed it to sea and set it adrift, leaving the wretched men, bound as they were, to perish by famine, or by the winds and waves, as chance should determine. But fate so ordered it, that a boat belonging to the Laird of MacLeod

D

fell in with that which had the captives on board, and
brought them in safety to the laird's castle of Dunvegan
in Skye, where they complained of the injury which
they had sustained from the MacDonalds of Eigg.
MacLeod, in a great rage, put to sea with his galleys,
manned by a large body of his people, which the men
of Eigg could not entertain any rational hope of resisting.
Learning that their incensed enemy was approaching
with superior forces, and deep vows of revenge, the
inhabitants, who knew they had no mercy to expect at
MacLeod's hands, resolved, as the best chance of safety
in their power, to conceal themselves in a large cavern
on the seashore.

This place was particularly well calculated for that
purpose. The entrance resembles that of a fox-earth,
being an opening so small that a man cannot enter
save by creeping on hands and knees. A rill of water
falls from the top of the rock, and serves, or rather
served at the period we speak of, wholly to conceal the
aperture. A stranger, even when apprised of the existence
of such a cave, would find the greatest difficulty in dis-
covering the entrance. Within, the cavern rises to a great
height, and the floor is covered with white dry sand. It
is extensive enough to contain a great number of people.
The whole inhabitants of Eigg, who, with their wives
and families, amounted to nearly two hundred souls,
took refuge within its precincts.

MacLeod arrived with his armament, and landed on
the island, but could discover no one on whom to wreak
his vengeance—all was desert. The MacLeods destroyed
the huts of the islanders, and plundered what property
they could discover, but the vengeance of the chieftain
could not be satisfied with such petty injuries. He knew
that the inhabitants must either have fled in their boats

to one of the islands possessed by the MacDonalds, or that they must be concealed somewhere in Eigg. After making a strict but unsuccessful search for two days, MacLeod had appointed the third to leave his anchorage, when, in the grey of the morning, one of the seamen beheld from the deck of his galley the figure of a man on the island. This was a spy whom the MacDonalds, impatient of their confinement in the cavern, had imprudently sent out to see whether MacLeod had retired or no. The poor fellow, when he saw himself discovered, endeavoured, by doubling, after the manner of a hare or fox, to obliterate the track of his footsteps on the snow, and prevent its being discovered where he had re-entered the cavern. But all the arts he could use were fruitless; the invaders again landed, and tracked him to the entrance of the den.

MacLeod then summoned those who were within it, and called upon them to deliver up the individuals who had maltreated his men, to be disposed of at his pleasure. The MacDonalds, still confident in the strength of their fastness, which no assailant could enter but on hands and knees, refused to surrender their clansmen.

MacLeod next commenced a dreadful work of indiscriminate vengeance. He caused his people, by means of a ditch cut above the top of the rock, to turn away the stream of water which fell over the entrance of the cavern. This being done, the MacLeods collected all the combustibles which could be found on the island, particularly turf and quantities of dry heather, piled them up against the aperture, and maintained an immense fire for many hours, until the smoke, penetrating into the inmost recesses of the cavern, stifled to death every creature within. There is no doubt of the truth of this story, dreadful as it is.

The MacLeans, in like manner, a bold and hardy race, who, originally followers of the Lords of the Isles, had assumed independence, seized upon great part both of the isle of Mull and the still more valuable island of Islay, and made war on the MacDonalds with various success. There is a story belonging to this clan, which I may tell you, as giving another striking picture of the manners of the Hebrideans.

The chief of the clan, MacLean of Duart, in the isle of Mull, had a son who received the name of Allan-a-Sop, by which he was distinguished from others of his clan. As his father and mother were not married, Allan was of course illegitimate, and had no inheritance to look for, save that which he might win for himself.

But the beauty of the boy's mother having captivated a man of rank in the clan, called MacLean of Torloisk, he married her, and took her to reside with him at his castle of Torloisk, situated on the shores of the sound, or small strait of the sea, which divides the smaller island of Ulva from that of Mull. Allan-a-Sop paid his mother frequent visits at her new residence, and she was naturally glad to see the poor boy, both from affection, and on account of his personal strength and beauty, which distinguished him above other youths of his age. But she was obliged to confer marks of her attachment on him as privately as she could, for Allan's visits were by no means so acceptable to her husband as to herself. Indeed, Torloisk liked so little to see the lad, that he determined to put some affront on him, which should prevent his returning to the castle for some time. An opportunity for executing his purpose soon occurred.

The lady one morning, looking from the window, saw her son coming wandering down the hill, and hastened to put a girdle cake upon the fire, that he might have hot bread for breakfast. Something called her out of the apartment after making this preparation, and her husband, entering at the same time, saw at once what she had been about, and determined to give the boy such a reception as should disgust him for the future. He snatched the cake from the girdle, thrust it into his step-son's hands, which he forcibly closed on the scalding bread, saying, "Here, Allan—here is a cake which your mother has got ready for your breakfast." Allan's hands were severely burnt; and, being a sharp-witted and proud boy, he resented this mark of his step-father's ill-will, and came not again to Torloisk.

At this time the western seas were covered with the vessels of pirates, who, not unlike the Sea-Kings of Denmark at an early period, sometimes settled and made conquests on the islands. Allan-a-Sop was young, strong and brave to desperation. He entered as a mariner on board of one of these ships, and in process of time obtained the command, first of one galley, then of a small flotilla, with which he sailed round the seas and collected considerable plunder, until his name became both feared and famous. At length he proposed to himself to pay a visit to his mother, whom he had not seen for many years; and setting sail for this purpose, he anchored one morning in the sound of Ulva, and in front of the house of Torloisk. His mother was dead, but his stepfather, to whom he was now as much an object of fear as he had been formerly of aversion, hastened to the shore to receive his formidable stepson, with great affectation of kindness and interest in his prosperity; while Allan-a-Sop, who, though very rough and hasty, does not appear to have been sullen or vindictive, seemed to take his kind reception in good part.

The crafty old man succeeded so well, as he thought,

in securing Allan's friendship, and obliterating all recollections of the former affront put on him, that he began to think it possible to employ his stepson in executing his own private revenge upon MacQuarrie of Ulva, with whom, as was usual between such neighbours, he had some feud. With this purpose, he offered what he called the following good advice to his son-in-law: "My dear Allan, you have now wandered over the seas long enough; it is time you should have some footing upon land, a castle to protect yourself in winter, a village and cattle for your men, and a harbour to lay up your galleys. Now, here is the island of Ulva, near at hand, which lies ready for your occupation, and it will cost you no trouble, save that of putting to death the present proprietor, the Laird of MacQuarrie, a useless old carle, who has cumbered the world long enough."

Allan-a-Sop thanked his stepfather for so happy a suggestion, which he declared he would put in execution forthwith. Accordingly, setting sail the next morning, he appeared before MacQuarrie's house an hour before noon. The old chief of Ulva was much alarmed at the menacing apparition of so many galleys, and his anxiety was not lessened by the news that they were commanded by the redoubted Allan - a - Sop. Having no effectual means of resistance, MacQuarrie, who was a man of shrewd sense, saw no alternative save that of receiving the invaders, whatever might be their purpose, with all outward demonstrations of joy and satisfaction; the more especially as he recollected having taken some occasional notice of Allan during his early youth, which he now resolved to make the most of. Accordingly, MacQuarrie caused immediate preparations to be made for a banquet as splendid as circumstances admitted, hastened down to the shore to meet the rover, and welcomed him to Ulva with such an appearance of sincerity, that the pirate found it impossible to pick any quarrel which might afford a pretence for executing the violent purpose which he had been led to meditate.

They feasted together the whole day; and, in the evening, as Allan-a-Sop was about to retire to his ships, he thanked the laird for his hospitality, but remarked, with a sigh, that it had cost him very dear. "How can that be," said MacQuarrie, "when I bestowed this entertainment upon you in free good will?"—"It is true, my friend," replied the pirate, "but then it has quite disconcerted the purpose for which I came hither; which was to put you to death, my good friend, and seize upon your house and island, and so settle myself in the world. It would have been very convenient for me, this island of Ulva; but your friendly reception has rendered it impossible for me to execute my purpose: so that I must be a wanderer on the seas for some time longer." Whatever MacQuarrie felt at learning he had been so near to destruction, he took care to show no emotion save surprise, and replied to his visitor, "My dear Allan, who was it that put into your mind so unkind a purpose towards your old friend; for I am sure it never arose from your own generous nature? It must have been old Torloisk, who made such an indifferent husband to your mother, and such an unfriendly stepfather to you when you were a helpless boy; but now, when he sees you a bold and powerful leader, he desires to make a quarrel betwixt you and those who were the friends of your youth. If you consider this matter rightly, Allan, you will see that the estate and harbour of Torloisk lie to the full as conveniently for you as those of Ulva, and that, if you are disposed (as is very natural) to make a settlement by force, it is much better it should be at the expense of the old churl, who never showed you kindness or countenance, than at that of a friend like me, who always loved and honoured you."

Allan-a-Sop was struck with the justice of this reasoning; and the old offence of his scalded fingers was suddenly recalled to his mind. "It is very true what you say, MacQuarrie," he replied; "and, besides, I have not forgotten what a hot breakfast my stepfather treated me to one morning. Farewell for the present; you shall soon hear news of me from the other side of the sound." Having said thus much, the pirate got on board, and, commanding his men to unmoor the galleys, sailed back to Torloisk, and prepared to land in arms. MacLean hastened to meet him, in expectation to hear of the death of his enemy, MacQuarrie. But Allan greeted him in a very different manner from what he expected. "You hoary old traitor," he said, "you instigated my simple good nature to murder a better man than yourself! But have you forgotten how you scorched my fingers twenty years ago with a burning cake? The day is come that that breakfast must be paid for." So saying, he dashed out the old man's brains with a battle-axe, took possession of his castle and property, and established there a distinguished branch of the clan of MacLean.

It is told of another of these western chiefs, who is said, upon the whole, to have been a kind and good-natured man, that he was subjected to repeated risk and injury by the treachery of an ungrateful nephew, who attempted to surprise his castle, in order to put his uncle to death, and obtain for himself the command of the tribe. Being detected on the first occasion, and brought before his uncle as a prisoner, the chief dismissed him unharmed; with a warning, however, not to repeat the offence, since, if he did so, he would cause him to be put to a death so fearful that all Scotland should ring with it. The wicked young man persevered, and renewed his attempts against his uncle's castle and life. Falling a second time into the hands of the offended chieftain, the prisoner had reason to term him as good as his word. He was confined in the pit, or dungeon, of the castle, a deep dark vault, to which there was no access save through a hole in the roof. He was left without food, till his appetite grew voracious; the more so, as he had reason to apprehend that it was intended to starve him to death. But the vengeance of his uncle was of a more refined character. The stone which covered the aperture in the roof was lifted, and a quantity of salt beef let down to the prisoner, who devoured it eagerly. When he had glutted himself with this food, and expected to be supplied with liquor, to quench the raging thirst which the diet had excited, a cup was slowly lowered down, which, when he eagerly grasped it, he found to be empty! Then they rolled the stone on the opening in the vault, and left the captive to perish by thirst, the most dreadful of all deaths.

DONALD OF THE HAMMER

THE size and position of the Highlands of Scotland rendered them much less susceptible of improvement than the Border districts, which, far less extensive, and less difficult of access, were (after 1603) placed between two civilised and peaceful countries, instead of being the frontier of two hostile lands.

The Highlanders, on the contrary, continued the same series of wars among themselves, and incursions upon their Lowland neighbours, which had distinguished them ever since the dawn of their history. Military adventure, in one form or other, was their delight as well as their employment, and all works of industry were considered as unworthy the dignity of a mountaineer. Even the necessary task of raising a scanty crop of barley was assigned to the aged, and to the women and children. The men thought of nothing but hunting and war. I will give you an account of a Highland chieftain, in character and practice not very different from that of Allan-a-Sop, the Hebridean.

The Stewarts, who inhabited the district of Appin, in the West Highlands, were a numerous and warlike clan. Appin is the title of the chief of the clan. The second branch of the family was that of Invernahyle. The founder, a second son of the house of Appin, was called by the uncommon epithet of *Saioleach* or the *Peaceful*. One of his neighbours was the Lord of Dunstaffnage, called Cailen Uaine, or Green Colin, from the green colour which predominated in his tartan. This Green Colin surprised the peaceful Laird of Invernahyle, assassinated him, burnt his house, and destroyed his whole family, excepting an infant at the breast. This infant did not owe its safety to the mercy of Green Colin, but to the activity and presence of mind of its nurse. Finding she could not escape the pursuit of that chief's attendants, the faithful nurse determined to provide for the safety of her foster-child, whose life she knew was aimed at, in the only manner which remained. She therefore hid the infant in a small fissure, or cave, of a rock, and as the only means she had of supplying him with subsistence, hung by a string round his neck a large piece of lard, in the faint hope that instinct might induce the child to employ it as a means of subsistence. The poor woman had only time to get a little way from the place where she had concealed her charge, when she was made prisoner by the pursuers. As she denied any knowledge where the child was, they dismissed her as a person of no consequence, but not until they had kept her two or three days in close confinement, menacing her with death unless she would discover what she had done with the infant.

When she found herself at liberty and unobserved, she went to the hole in which she had concealed her charge, with little hope save of finding such relics as wolves, wild-cats, or birds of prey might have left after feasting upon its flesh, but still with the pious wish to consign the remains of her *dault*, or foster-child, to some place of Christian burial. But her joy and surprise were extreme to find the infant still alive and well, having lived during her absence by sucking the lard, which it had reduced to a very small morsel, scarce larger than a hazel nut. The delighted nurse made all haste to escape with her charge to the neighbouring district of Moidart, of which she was a native, being the wife of the smith of the clan of MacDonald, to whom that country belonged. The mother of the infant thus miraculously rescued had also been a daughter of this tribe.

To ensure the safety of her foster-child, the nurse persuaded her husband to bring it up as their own son. The smith, you must remark, of a Highland tribe was a person of considerable consequence. His skill in forging armour and weapons was usually united with dexterity in using them, and with the strength of body which his profession required. If I recollect right, the smith usually ranked as third officer in the chief's household. The young Donald Stewart, as he grew up, was distinguished for great personal strength. He became skilful in his foster-father's art, and so powerful, that he could, it is said, wield two fore-hammers, one in each hand, for hours together. From this circumstance, he gained the name of *Donuil nan Ord*, that is, Donald of the Hammer, by which he was all his life distinguished.

When he attained the age of twenty-one, Donald's foster-father, the smith, observing that his courage and enterprise equalled his personal strength, thought fit to discover to him the secret of his birth, the injuries which he had received from Green Colin of Dunstaffnage, and the pretensions which he had to the property of Invernahyle, now in the possession of the man who had slain his father and usurped his inheritance. He concluded his discovery by presenting to his beloved foster-child his own six sons to be his followers and defenders for life and death, and his assistants in the recovery of his patrimony.

Law of every description was unknown in the Highlands. Young Donald proceeded in his enterprise by hostile measures. In addition to his six foster-brethren, he got some assistance from his mother's kindred, and levied among the old adherents of his father, and his kinsmen of the house of Appin, such additional force, that he was able to give battle to Green Colin, whom he defeated and slew, regaining at the same time his father's house and estate of Invernahyle. This success had its dangers; for it placed the young chief in feud with all the families of the powerful clan of Campbell, to which the slain Dunstaffnage belonged by alliance at least; for Green Colin and his ancestors had assumed the name, and ranked themselves under the banner, of this formidable clan, although originally they were chieftains of a different and independent race. The feud became more deadly when, not satisfied with revenging himself on the immediate authors of his early misfortune, Donald made inroads on the Campbells in their own dominions; in evidence of which his historian quotes a verse to this purpose:

> Donald of the Smithy, the Son of the Hammer,
> Filled the banks of Lochawe with mourning and clamour.

At length the powerful Earl of Argyle resented the repeated injuries which were offered to his clansmen and kindred. The Stewarts of Appin refused to support their kinsman against an enemy so formidable, and insisted that he should seek for peace with the Earl. So that Donald, left to himself, and sensible that he was unable to withstand the force which might be brought against him by this mighty chief, endeavoured to propitiate the Earl's favour by placing himself in his hands.

Stewart went, accordingly, with only a single attendant, towards Inverary, the castle of Argyle, and met with the Earl himself at some distance in the open fields.

Donald of the Hammer showed on this occasion that it
was not fear which had induced him to this step. Being
a man of ready wit, and a poet, which was an accomplish-
ment high in the estimation of the Highlanders, he opened
the conference with an extempore verse, which intimated
a sort of defiance, rather like the language of a man that
cared not what might befall him, than one who craved
mercy or asked forgiveness.

> Son of dark Colin, thou dangerous earl,
>   Small is the boon that I crave at thy hand;
> Enough, if in safety from bondage and peril,
>   Thou let'st me return to my kindred and land.

The Earl was too generous to avail himself of the
advantage which Invernahyle's confidence had afforded
him, but he could not abstain from maintaining the
conversation, thus begun, in a gibing tone. Donuil nan
Ord was harsh-featured, and had a custom, allied to his
mode of education and the haughtiness of his character,
of throwing back his head and laughing loudly with his
mouth wide open. In ridicule of this peculiarity, in which
Donald had indulged repeatedly, Argyle, or one of his
attendants, pointed out to his observation a rock in the
neighbourhood, which bore a singular resemblance to
a human face, with a large mouth much thrown back,
and open as if laughing a horse-laugh. "Do you see
yonder crag?" said the Earl to Donald of the Hammer:
"it is called *Gaire Granda,* or the *Ugly Laugh.*" Donald
felt the intended gibe, and as Argyle's lady was a hard-
favoured and haughty woman, he replied, without
hesitation, in a verse like the following:

> Ugly the sneer of yon cliff of the hill,
>   Nature has stamp'd the grim laugh on the place;
> Would you seek for a grimmer and uglier still,
>   You will find it at home in your countess's face.

Argyle took the raillery of Donald in good part, but would not make peace with him until he agreed to make two *creaghs*, or inroads, one on Moidart, and one on Athole. It seems probable that the purpose of Argyle was to engage his troublesome neighbour in a feud with other clans to whom he bore no good-will; for whether he of the Hammer fell or was successful, the Earl, in either event, would gain a certain advantage. Donald accepted peace with the Campbells on these terms.

On his return home, Donald communicated to Mac-Donald of Moidart the engagement he had come under; and that chieftain, his mother's kinsman and ally, concerted that Invernahyle and his band should plunder certain villages in Moidart, the inhabitants of which had offended him and on whom he desired chastisement should be inflicted. The incursion of Donald the Hammerer punished them to some purpose, and so far he fulfilled his engagement to Argyle, without making an enemy of his own kinsman. With the Athole men, as more distant and unconnected with him, Donald stood on less ceremony, and made more than one successful creagh upon them. His name was now established as one of the most formidable marauders known in the Highlands, and a very bloody action which he sustained against the family of the Grahams of Monteith made him still more dreaded.

The Earls of Monteith, you must know, had a castle situated upon an island in the lake, or loch, as it is called, of the same name. But though this residence, which occupied almost the whole of the islet upon which its ruins still exist, was a strong and safe place of abode, and adapted accordingly to such perilous times, it had this inconvenience, that the stables, cow-houses, poultry-yard, and other domestic offices, were necessarily separated from the castle, and situated on the mainland, as it would have been impossible to be constantly transporting the animals belonging to the establishment to and fro from the shore to the island. These offices, therefore, were constructed on the banks of the lake, and in some sort defenceless.

It happened upon a time that there was to be a great entertainment in the castle, and a number of the Grahams were assembled. The occasion, it is said, was a marriage in the family. To prepare for this feast, much provision was got ready, and in particular a great deal of poultry had been collected. While the feast was preparing, an unhappy chance brought Donald of the Hammer to the side of the lake, returning at the head of a band of hungry followers, whom he was conducting homewards to the West Highlands, after some of his usual excursions into Stirlingshire. Seeing so much good victuals ready, and being possessed of an excellent appetite, the Western Highlanders neither asked questions nor waited for an invitation, but devoured all the provisions that had been prepared for the Grahams, and then went on their way rejoicing, through the difficult and dangerous path which leads from the banks of the loch of Monteith, through the mountains, to the side of Loch Katrine.

The Grahams were filled with the highest indignation. No one in those fierce times was so contemptible as an individual who would suffer himself to be plundered without exacting satisfaction and revenge, and the loss of their dinner probably aggravated the sense of the insults entertained by the guests. The company who were assembled at the castle of Monteith, headed by the Earl himself, hastily took to their boats, and, disembarking on the northern side of the lake, pursued with all speed the marauders and their leader. They came up with

Donald's party in the gorge of a pass, near a rock called Craig-Vad, or the Wolf's Cliff. Here the Grahams called, with loud insults, on the Appin men to stand, and one of them, in allusion to the execution which had been done amongst the poultry, exclaimed in verse:

> They're brave gallants, these Appin men,
> To twist the throat of cock and hen!

Donald instantly replied to the reproach:

> And if we be of Appin's line,
> We'll twist a goose's neck in thine.

So saying, he shot the unlucky scoffer with an arrow. The battle then began, and was continued with much fury till night. The Earl of Monteith and many of his noble kinsmen fell, while Donald, favoured by darkness, escaped with a single attendant. The Grahams obtained, from the cause of the quarrel, the nickname of Gramoch an Garrigh, or Grahams of the Hens: although they certainly lost no honour in the encounter, having fought like game-cocks.

Donald of the Hammer was twice married. His second marriage was highly displeasing to his eldest son, whom he had by his first wife. This young man, whose name was Duncan, seems to have partaken rather of the disposition of his grandfather, Alister *Saioleach*, or the Peaceful, than of the turbulent spirit of his father the Hammerer. He quitted the family mansion in displeasure at his father's second marriage, and went to a farm called Inverfalla, which his father had bestowed upon his nurse in reward for her eminent services. Duncan took up his abode with this valued connection of the family, who was now in the extremity of old age, and amused himself with attempting to improve the cultivation of the farm; a task which not only was considered as below the dignity of a Highland gentleman, but even regarded as the last degree of degradation.

The idea of his son's occupying himself with agricultural operations struck so much shame and anger into the heart of Donald the Hammerer, that his resentment against him became ungovernable. At length, as he walked by his own side of the river, and looked towards Inverfalla, he saw, to his extreme displeasure, a number of men employed in digging and levelling the soil for some intended crop. Soon after, he had the additional mortification to see his son come out and mingle with the workmen, as if giving them directions; and, finally, beheld him take the spade out of an awkward fellow's hand, and dig a little himself to show him how to use it. This last act of degeneracy drove the Hammerer frantic; he seized a curragh, or boat covered with hides, which was near, jumped into it, and pushed across the stream, with the determination of destroying the son who had, in his opinion, brought such unutterable disgrace upon his family. The poor agriculturist seeing his father approach in such haste, and having a shrewd guess of the nature of his parental intentions, fled into the house and hid himself. Donald followed with his drawn weapon; but, deceived by passion and darkness, he plunged his sword into the body of one whom he saw lying on the bed-clothes. Instead of his son, for whom the blow was intended, it lighted on the old foster-mother, to whom he owed his life in infancy and education in youth, and slew her on the spot. After this misfortune, Donald became deeply affected with remorse; and giving up all his estates to his children, he retired to the Abbey of St. Columba, in Iona, passed the remainder of his days as a monk, and died at the age of eighty-seven.

JOHN BROWN, THE CHRISTIAN CARRIER

THERE lived at this gloomy period, at a place called Preshill, or Priesthill, in Lanarkshire, a man named John Brown, a carrier by profession, and called, from his zealous religious principles, the Christian Carrier. This person had been out with the insurgents at Bothwell Bridge, and was for other reasons amenable to the cruelty of the existing laws. On a morning of May 1685, Peden, one of the Cameronian ministers, whom Brown had sheltered in his house, took his leave of his host and his wife, repeating twice, "Poor woman! a fearful morning —a dark and misty morning!"—words which were afterwards believed to be prophetic of calamity. When Peden was gone, Brown left his house with a spade in his hand for his ordinary labour, when he was suddenly surrounded and arrested by a band of horse, with Claverhouse at their head. Although the prisoner had a hesitation in his speech on ordinary occasions, he answered the questions which were put to him in this extremity with such composure and firmness that Claverhouse asked whether he was a preacher. He was answered in the negative. "If he has not preached," said Claverhouse, "mickle hath he prayed in his time.—But betake you now to your prayers for the last time" (addressing the sufferer), "for you shall presently die." The poor man kneeled down and prayed with zeal; and when he was touching on the political state of the country, and praying that Heaven would spare a remnant, Claverhouse, interrupting him, said, "I gave you leave to pray, and you are preaching."—"Sir," answered the prisoner, turning towards his judge on his knees, "you know nothing either of preaching or praying, if you call what I now say preaching":—then continued without confusion. When his devotions were ended, Claverhouse commanded him to bid good-night to his wife and children. Brown turned towards them, and, taking his wife by the hand, told her that the hour was come which he had spoken of, when he first asked her consent to marry him. The poor woman answered firmly, "In this cause I am willing to resign you."—"Then have I nothing to do save to die," he replied; "and I thank God I have been in a frame to meet death for many years." He was shot dead by a party of soldiers at the end of his own house; and although his wife was of a nervous habit, and used to become sick at the sight of blood, she had on this occasion strength enough to support the dreadful scene without fainting or confusion, only her eyes dazzled when the carabines were fired. While her husband's dead body lay stretched before him, Claverhouse asked her what she thought of her husband now. "I ever thought much of him," she replied, "and now more than ever."—"It were but justice," said Claverhouse, "to lay thee beside him."—"I doubt not," she replied, "that if you were permitted, your cruelty would carry you that length. But how will you answer for this morning's work?"—"To man I can be answerable," said Claverhouse, "and Heaven I will take in my own hand." He then mounted his horse and marched, and left her with the corpse of her husband lying beside her, and her fatherless infant in her arms. "She placed the child on the ground," says the narrative with scriptural simplicity, "tied up the corpse's head, and straighted the limbs, and covered him with her plaid, and sat down and wept over him."

THE DEFENCE OF THE BASS

AT length the last faint embers of civil war died away throughout Scotland. The last place which held out for King James II. was the strong island and castle in the Firth of Forth, called the Bass. This singular rock rises perpendicularly out of the sea. The surface is pasture land sloping to the brink of a tremendous precipice, which on all sides sinks sheer down into the stormy ocean. There is no anchorage ground on any point near the rock; and although it is possible in the present state of the island to go ashore (not without danger, however), and to ascend by a steep path to the table-land on the top of the crag, yet at the time of the Revolution a strong castle defended the landing-place, and the boats belonging to the garrison were lowered into the sea, or heaved up into the castle, by means of the engine called a crane. Access was thus difficult to friends, and impossible to enemies.

This sequestered and inaccessible spot, the natural shelter and abode of gannets, gulls, and sea-fowl of all descriptions, had been, as I have before noticed, converted into a state prison during the reigns of Charles II. and James II.; and was often the melancholy abode of the nonconformists, who were prisoners to Government. When the Revolution took place the Governor of the Bass held out from 1688 to 1690, when he surrendered the island and castle to King William. They were shortly after recovered for King James by some Jacobite officers, who, sent thither as prisoners, contrived to surprise and overpower the garrison, and again bade defiance to the new Government. They received supplies of provisions from their Jacobite friends on shore, and exercised, by means of their boats, a sort of privateering warfare on such merchant vessels as entered the firth. A squadron of English ships of war was sent to reduce the place, which, in their attempt to batter the castle, did so little damage, and received so much, that the siege was given up, or rather converted into a strict blockade. The punishment of death was denounced by the Scottish Government against all who should attempt to supply the island with provisions; and a gentleman named Trotter, having been convicted of such an attempt, was condemned to death, and a gallows erected opposite to the Bass, that the garrison might witness his fate. The execution was interrupted for the time by a cannon-shot from the island, to the great terror of the assistants, amongst whom the bullet lighted; but no advantage accrued to Trotter, who was put to death elsewhere. The intercourse between the island and the shore was in this manner entirely cut off. Shortly afterwards the garrison became so weak for want of provisions that they were unable to man the crane by which they launched out and got in their boats. They were thus obliged finally to surrender, but not till reduced to an allowance of two ounces of rusk to each man per day. They were admitted to honourable terms, with the testimony of having done their duty like brave men.

THE MASSACRE OF GLENCOE

MacIan of Glencoe (this was the patronymic title of the chief of this clan) was a man of a stately and venerable person and aspect. He possessed both courage and sagacity, and was accustomed to be listened to by the neighbouring chieftains, and to take a lead in their deliberations. MacIan had been deeply engaged both in the campaign of Killiecrankie and in that which followed under General Buchan; and when the insurgent Highland chiefs held a meeting with the Earl of Breadalbane, at a place called Auchallader, in the month of July 1691, for the purpose of arranging an armistice, MacIan was present with the rest, and, it is said, taxed Breadalbane with the design of retaining a part of the money lodged in his hands for the pacification of the Highlands. The earl retorted with vehemence, and charged MacIan with a theft of cattle, committed upon some of his lands by a party from Glencoe. Other causes of offence took place, in which old feuds were called to recollection; and MacIan was repeatedly heard to say, he dreaded mischief from no man so much as from the Earl of Breadalbane. Yet this unhappy chief was rash enough to stand out to the last moment, and decline to take advantage of King William's indemnity, till the time appointed by the proclamation was wellnigh expired.

The displeasure of the Earl of Breadalbane seems speedily to have communicated itself to the Master of Stair, who, in his correspondence with Lieutenant-Colonel Hamilton, then commanding in the Highlands, expresses the greatest resentment against MacIan of Glencoe, for having, by his interference, marred the bargain between Breadalbane and the Highland chiefs. Accordingly, in a letter of 3rd December, the secretary intimated that Government was determined to destroy utterly some of the clans, in order to terrify the others; and he hoped that, by standing out and refusing to submit under the indemnity, the MacDonalds of Glencoe would fall into the net,—which meant that they would afford a pretext for their extirpation. This letter is dated a month before the time limited by the indemnity; so long did these bloody thoughts occupy the mind of this unprincipled statesman.

Ere the term of mercy expired, however, MacIan's own apprehensions, or the advice of friends, dictated to him the necessity of submitting to the same conditions which others had embraced, and he went with his principal followers to take the oath of allegiance to King William. This was a very brief space before the 1st January, when, by the terms of the proclamation, the opportunity of claiming the indemnity was to expire. MacIan was, therefore, much alarmed to find that Colonel Hill, the Governor of Fort William, to whom he tendered his oath of allegiance, had no power to receive it, being a military, and not a civil officer. Colonel Hill, however, sympathised with the distress and even tears of the old chieftain, and gave him a letter to Sir Colin Campbell of Ardkinglas, Sheriff of Argyleshire, requesting him to receive the "lost sheep," and administer the oath to him, that he might have the advantage of the indemnity, though so late in claiming it.

MacIan hastened from Fort William to Inverary, without even turning aside to his own house, though he passed within a mile of it. But the roads, always very bad, were now rendered almost impassable by a storm of snow; so that, with all the speed the unfortunate chieftain could exert, the fatal first of January was past before he reached Inverary.

The sheriff, however, seeing that MacIan had complied with the spirit of the statute, in tendering his submission within the given period, under the sincere, though mistaken belief, that he was applying to the person ordered to receive it; and considering also, that, but for the tempestuous weather, it would after all have been offered in presence of the proper law-officer, did not hesitate to administer the oath of allegiance, and sent off an express to the Privy Council, containing an attestation of MacIan's having taken the oaths, and a full explanation of the circumstances which had delayed his doing so until the lapse of the appointed period. The sheriff also wrote to Colonel Hill what he had done, and requested that he would take care that Glencoe should not be annoyed by any military parties until the pleasure of the Council should be known, which he could not doubt would be favourable.

MacIan, therefore, returned to his own house, and resided there, as he supposed in safety, under the protection of the Government to which he had sworn allegiance. That he might merit this protection, he convoked his clan, acquainted them with his submission, and commanded them to live peaceably, and give no cause of offence, under pain of his displeasure.

In the meantime, the vindictive secretary of state had procured orders from his sovereign respecting the measures to be followed with such of the chiefs as should not have taken the oaths within the term prescribed. The first of these orders, dated 11th January, contained peremptory directions for military execution, by fire and sword, against all who should not have made their submission within the time appointed. It was, however, provided, in order to avoid driving them to desperation, that there was still to remain a power of granting mercy to those clans who, even after the time was past, should still come in and submit themselves. Such were the terms of the first Royal warrant, in which Glencoe was not expressly named.

It seems afterwards to have occurred to Stair, that Glencoe and his tribe would be sheltered under this mitigation of the intended severities, since he had already come in and tendered his allegiance, without waiting for the menace of military force. A second set of instructions were therefore made out on the 16th January. These held out the same indulgence to other clans who should submit themselves at the very last hour (a hypocritical pretext, for there existed none which stood in such a predicament), but they closed the gate of mercy against the devoted MacIan, who had already done all that was required of others. The words are remarkable: "As for MacIan of Glencoe and that tribe, if they can be well distinguished from the rest of the Highlanders, it will be proper for the vindication of public justice, to extirpate that set of thieves."

You will remark the hypocritical clemency and real cruelty of these instructions, which profess a readiness to extend mercy to those who needed it not (for all the other Highlanders had submitted within the limited time), and deny it to Glencoe, the only man who had not been able literally to comply with the proclamation, though in all fair construction, he had done what it required.

Under what pretence or colouring King William's authority was obtained for such cruel instructions, it would be in vain to inquire. The Sheriff of Argyle's letter had never been produced before the Council; and the certificate of MacIan's having taken the oath was blotted out, and, in the Scottish phrase, deleted from the books of the Privy Council. It seems probable therefore that the fact of that chief's submission was altogether concealed from the king, and that he was held out in the light of a desperate and incorrigible leader of banditti, who was the main obstacle to the peace of the Highlands; but if we admit that William acted under such misrepresentations, deep blame will still attach to him for rashly issuing orders of an import so dreadful. It is remarkable that these fatal instructions are both superscribed and subscribed by the king himself, whereas in most state papers the sovereign only superscribes, and they are countersigned by the secretary of state, who is answerable for their tenor; a responsibility which Stair, on that occasion, was not probably ambitious of claiming.

The secretary's letters to the military officers, directing the mode of executing the king's orders, betray the deep and savage interest which he took personally in their tenor, and his desire that the bloody measure should be as general as possible. He dwelt in these letters upon the proper time and season for cutting off the devoted tribe. "The winter," he said, "is the only season in which the Highlanders cannot elude us, or carry their wives, children, and cattle, to the mountains. They cannot escape you; for what human constitution can then endure to be long out of house? This is the proper season to maul them, in the long dark nights." He could not suppress his joy that Glencoe had not come in within the term prescribed; and expresses his hearty wishes that others had followed the same course. He assured the soldiers that their powers should be ample; and he exacted from them proportional exertions. He entreated that the thieving tribe of Glencoe might be *rooted out* in earnest; and he was at pains to explain a phrase which is in itself terribly significant. He gave directions for securing every pass by which the victims could escape, and warned the soldiers that it were better to leave the thing unattempted, than fail to do it to purpose. "To plunder their lands, or drive off their cattle, would," say his letters, "be only to render them desperate; they must be all slaughtered, and the manner of execution must be sure, secret, and effectual."

These instructions, such as have been rarely penned in a Christian country, were sent to Colonel Hill, the Governor of Fort William, who, greatly surprised and grieved at their tenor, endeavoured for some time to evade the execution of them. At length, obliged by his situation to render obedience to the king's commands, he transmitted the orders to Lieutenant-Colonel Hamilton, directing him to take four hundred men of a Highland regiment belonging to the Earl of Argyle, and fulfil the royal mandate. Thus, to make what was intended yet worse, if possible, than it was in its whole tenor, the perpetration of this cruelty was committed to soldiers who were not only the countrymen of the proscribed, but the near neighbours, and some of them the close connections, of the MacDonalds of Glencoe. This is the more necessary to be remembered, because the massacre has unjustly been said to have been committed by English troops. The course of the bloody deed was as follows.

Before the end of January, a party of the Earl of Argyle's regiment, commanded by Captain Campbell of Glenlyon, approached Glencoe. MacIan's sons went out to meet them with a body of men, to demand whether they came as friends or foes. The officer replied, that they came as friends, being sent to take up their quarters for a short time in Glencoe, in order to relieve the garrison of Fort William, which was crowded with soldiers. On this they were welcomed with all the hospitality which the chief and his followers had the means of extending to them, and they resided for fifteen days amongst the unsuspecting MacDonalds, in the exchange of every species of kindness and civility. That the laws of domestic affection might be violated at the same time with those of humanity and hospitality, you are to understand that Alaster MacDonald, one of the sons of MacIan, was married to a niece of Glenlyon, who commanded the party of soldiers. It appears also, that the intended cruelty was to be exercised upon defenceless men: for the MacDonalds, though afraid of no other ill-treatment from their military guests, had supposed it possible the soldiers might have a commission to disarm them, and therefore had sent their weapons to a distance, where they might be out of reach of seizure.

Glenlyon's party had remained in Glencoe for fourteen or fifteen days, when he received orders from his commanding officer, Major Duncanson, expressed in a manner which shows him to have been the worthy agent of the cruel secretary. They were sent in conformity with orders of the same date, transmitted to Duncanson by Hamilton, directing that all the MacDonalds, under seventy years of age, were to be cut off, and that the *Government was not to be troubled with prisoners*. Duncanson's orders to Glenlyon were as follows:

You are hereby ordered to fall upon the rebels, and put all to the sword under seventy. You are to have especial care that the old fox and his cubs do on no account escape your hands; you are to secure all the avenues, that no man escape. This you are to put in execution at four in the morning precisely, and by that time, or very shortly after, I will strive to be at you with a stronger party. But if I do not come to you at four, you are not to tarry for me, but fall on. This is by the king's special command, for the good and safety of the country, that these miscreants be cut off root and branch. See that this be put into execution without either fear or favour, else you may expect to be treated as not true to the king or Government, nor a man fit to carry a commission in the king's service. Expecting that you will not fail in the fulfilling hereof, as you love yourself, I subscribe these with my hand,

                                    ROBERT DUNCANSON.

This order was dated 12th February, and addressed, "For their Majesties' service, to Captain Robert Campbell of Glenlyon."

This letter reached Glenlyon soon after it was written; and he lost no time in carrying the dreadful mandate into execution. In the interval, he did not abstain from any of those acts of familiarity which had lulled asleep the suspicions of his victims. He took his morning draught, as had been his practice every day since he came to the glen, at the house of Alaster MacDonald, MacIan's second son, who was married to his (Glenlyon's) niece. He, and two of his officers named Lindsay, accepted an invitation to dinner from MacIan himself, for the following day, on which they had determined he should never see the sun rise. To complete the sum of treachery, Glenlyon played at cards, in his own quarters, with the sons of MacIan, John and Alaster, both of whom were also destined for slaughter.

About four o'clock in the morning of 13th February the scene of blood began. A party, commanded by one of the Lindsays, came to MacIan's house and knocked for admittance, which was at once given. Lindsay, one of the expected guests at the family meal of the day, commanded this party, who instantly shot MacIan dead by his own bedside, as he was in the act of dressing himself, and giving orders for refreshments to be provided for his fatal visitors. His aged wife was stripped by the savage soldiery, who, at the same time, drew off the gold rings from her fingers with their teeth. She died the next day, distracted with grief, and the brutal treatment she had received. Several domestics and clansmen were killed at the same place.

The two sons of the aged chieftain had not been altogether so confident as their father respecting the peaceful and friendly purpose of their guests. They observed, on the evening preceding the massacre, that the sentinels were doubled, and the main guard strengthened. John, the elder brother, had even overheard the soldiers muttering amongst themselves, that they cared not about fighting the men of the glen fairly, but did not like the nature of the service they were engaged in; while others consoled themselves with the military logic, that their officers must be answerable for the orders given, they having no choice save to obey them. Alarmed with what had been thus observed and heard, the young men hastened to Glenlyon's quarters, where they found that officer and his men preparing their arms. On questioning him about these suspicious appearances, Glenlyon accounted for them by a story that he was bound on an expedition against some of Glengarry's men; and alluding to the circumstance of their alliance, which made his own cruelty more detestable, he added, "If anything evil had been intended, would I not have told Alaster and my niece?"

Reassured by this communication, the young men retired to rest, but were speedily awakened by an old domestic, who called on the two brothers to rise and fly for their lives. "Is it time for you," he said, "to be sleeping, when your father is murdered on his own hearth?"

Thus roused, they hurried out in great terror, and heard throughout the glen, wherever there was a place of human habitation, the shouts of the murderers, the report of the muskets, the screams of the wounded, and the groans of the dying. By their perfect knowledge of the scarce accessible cliffs amongst which they dwelt, they were enabled to escape observation, and fled to the southern access of the glen.

Meantime, the work of death proceeded with as little remorse as Stair himself could have desired. Even the slight mitigation of their orders respecting those above seventy years was disregarded by the soldiery in their indiscriminate thirst for blood, and several very aged and bedridden persons were slain amongst others. At the hamlet where Glenlyon had his own quarters, nine men, including his landlord, were bound and shot like felons; and one of them, MacDonald of Auchintriaten, had General Hill's passport in his pocket at the time. A fine lad of twenty had, by some glimpse of compassion on the part of the soldiers, been spared, when one Captain Drummond came up, and demanding why the orders were transgressed in that particular, caused him instantly to be put to death. A boy, of five or six years old, clung to Glenlyon's knees, entreating for mercy, and offering to become his servant for life, if he would spare him. Glenlyon was moved; but the same Drummond stabbed the child with his dirk, while he was in this agony of supplication.

At a place called Auchnaion, one Barber, a sergeant, with a party of soldiers, fired on a group of nine Mac-Donalds, as they were assembled round their morning fire, and killed four of them. The owner of the house, a brother of the slain Auchintriaten, escaped unhurt, and expressed a wish to be put to death rather in the

open air than within the house. "For your bread which
I have eaten," answered Barber, "I will grant the
request." MacDonald was dragged to the door accordingly; but he was an active man, and when the soldiers
were presenting their firelocks to shoot him, he cast his
plaid over their faces, and taking advantage of the
confusion, broke from them, and escaped up the glen.

The alarm being now general, many other persons,
male and female, attempted their escape in the same
manner as the two sons of MacIan and the person last
mentioned. Flying from their burning huts, and from
their murderous visitors, the half-naked fugitives committed themselves to a winter morning of darkness, snow,
and storm, amidst a wilderness the most savage in the
West Highlands, having a bloody death behind them,
and before them tempest, famine, and desolation.
Bewildered in the snow-wreaths, several sank to rise
no more. But the severities of the storm were tender
mercies compared to the cruelty of their persecutors.
The great fall of snow, which proved fatal to several
of the fugitives, was the means of saving the remnant
that escaped. Major Duncanson, agreeably to the plan
expressed in his orders to Glenlyon, had not failed to put
himself in motion, with four hundred men, on the evening
preceding the slaughter; and had he reached the eastern
passes out of Glencoe by four in the morning, as he
calculated, he must have intercepted and destroyed all
those who took that only way of escape from Glenlyon
and his followers. But as this reinforcement arrived so
late as eleven in the forenoon, they found no MacDonald
alive in Glencoe, save an old man of eighty whom they
slew; and after burning such houses as were yet uncon-
sumed, they collected the property of the tribe, consisting
of twelve hundred head of cattle and horses, besides

E

goats and sheep, and drove them off to the garrison of Fort William.

Thus ended this horrible deed of massacre. The number of persons murdered was thirty-eight; those who escaped might amount to a hundred and fifty males, who, with the women and children of the tribe, had to fly more than twelve miles through rocks and wildernesses, ere they could reach any place of safety or shelter.

THE ESCAPE OF PRINCE CHARLES

THE first in rank, in misfortune, and in the temerity which led to the civil war, was unquestionably Charles Edward himself. A reward of £30,000 was offered for the discovery and seizure of this last scion of a royal line. It was imagined, that in a country so poor as the Highlands, lawless in a sense, so far as the law of property was concerned, and where the people were supposed to be almost proverbially rapacious, a much smaller reward would have insured the capture of the Pretender to the throne. His escape, however, so long delayed, and effected through so many difficulties, has been often commemorated as a brilliant instance of fidelity. I shall only here touch upon its general outlines, leaving you to acquire further details from other authors.

During the battle of Culloden Charles had his share of the dangers of the field. The cannon especially directed against his standard made some havoc among his guards, and killed one of his servants who held a led horse near to his person. The Prince himself was covered with the earth thrown up by the balls. He repeatedly endeavoured to rally his troops, and in the opinion of most who saw him did the duties of a brave and good commander. When he retreated from the field he was attended by a large body of horse, from whom, being perhaps under some doubt of their fidelity, he disengaged himself, by dismissing them on various errands, but particularly with instructions to warn the fugitives that they were to rendezvous at Ruthven, in Badenoch; for such had been the reckless resolution to fight, and such perhaps the confidence in victory, that no place of rendezvous had been announced to the army in case of defeat. Having dismissed the greater part of his horsemen, Charles retained around his person only a few of the Irish officers, who had been his constant followers, and whose faith he considered as less doubtful than that of the Scots, perhaps because they were themselves more loud in asserting it. He directed his flight to Gortuleg, where he understood Lord Lovat was residing. Perhaps he expected to find counsel in the renowned sagacity of this celebrated nobleman; perhaps he expected assistance from his power; for the Master of Lovat, and Cluny MacPherson, Lovat's son-in-law, were neither of them in the action of Culloden, but both in the act of bringing up strong reinforcements to the Prince's army, and on the march thither when the battle was lost.

Charles and Lovat met, for the first and last time, in mutual terror and embarrassment. The Prince exclaimed upon the distresses of Scotland; Lord Lovat had a more immediate sense of his own downfall. Having speedily found that neither counsel nor aid was to be obtained at Lovat's hands, the Prince only partook of some slight refreshment and rode on. He thought Gortuleg dangerous, as too near the victorious army, perhaps also he suspected the faith of its principal inmate. Invergarry, the castle of the Laird of Glengarry, was the next halt, where the chance success of a fisherman who had caught a brace of salmon afforded him a repast. The mansion-house suffered severely for the temporary reception of the Prince, being wasted and destroyed by the English soldiery with unusual rigour. From Invergarry the fugitive Prince penetrated into the West Highlands, and took up his abode in a village called Glenboisdale, very near the place where he had first landed. By this time he had totally renounced the further prosecution of his enterprise, his sanguine hopes being totally extinguished in the despair which attended his defeat. Charles despatched a message to those chiefs and soldiers who should rendezvous at Ruthven in obedience to his order, to acquaint them that, entertaining deep gratitude for their faithful attention and gallant conduct on all occasions, he was now under the necessity of recommending to them to look after their own safety, as he was compelled by circumstances to retire to France, from whence he hoped soon to return with succours.

Although not above one thousand men had attended at the appointed rendezvous, a great many of these thought that there was still hope of continuing the enterprise, and were disposed to remonstrate with the Prince on his resolution of abandoning it. Lord George Murray was of this opinion, and declared that, as for provisions, if he was entrusted with any direction, they should not want as long as there were cattle in the Highlands, or meal in the Lowlands. John Hay was despatched to wait upon the Prince, and entreat him even yet to resume his post at the head of his army.

It must be owned that these were the thoughts of desperate men; the enterprise had been despaired of by all sensible persons ever since the retreat from Stirling, if not since that from Derby. It was not to be supposed that an army with little hope of supplies or reinforcement, and composed of clans each independent of the others, and deprived of a great many of the best and boldest chiefs, while others, like Lochiel, were disabled by wounds, should adhere to an alliance in which there was no common object; and it is much more likely that, divided as they were by jealousies, they would have broken up as on former occasions, by each clan endeavouring to make its separate peace.

When John Hay, therefore, came to Charles at Glenboisdale, to convey Lord George Murray's expostulation and request, he received from the Prince a letter in answer, declaring, in stronger and plainer words, his determined intention to depart for France, from which he hoped soon to return with a powerful reinforcement. Each behaved according to his character. The stubborn resolution of Lord George Murray demonstrated the haughty obstinacy of his rough and indomitable character, which had long looked on the worst as an event likely to arrive, and was now ready to brave it; while the Prince, whose sanguine hopes could not be taught to anticipate a defeat, now regarded it with justice as an irretrievable evil.

From this time Charles must be regarded as providing for his own escape, and totally detached from the army which he lately commanded. With this view he embarked for the Long Island, on the coast of which he hoped to find a French vessel. Contrary winds, storms, disappointments of several sorts, attended with hardships to which he could be little accustomed, drove him from place to place in that island and its vicinity till he gained South Uist, where he was received by Clanranald, who, one of the first who joined the unfortunate Prince, was faithful to him in his distresses. Here, for security's sake, Charles was lodged in a forester's hut of the most miserable kind, called Corradale, about the centre of the wild mountain so named.

But every lurking-place was now closely sought after, and the islands in particular were strictly searched, for the purpose of securing the fugitive Prince, suspected of being concealed in their recesses. General Campbell sailed as far as the island of St. Kilda, which might well pass for the extremity of the habitable world. The simple inhabitants had but a very general idea of the war which had disturbed all Britain, except that it had arisen from some difference between their master, the Laird of MacLeod, and a female on the continent — probably some vague idea about the Queen of Hungary's concern in the war.

General Campbell, returning from Kilda, landed upon South Uist, with the purpose of searching the Long Island from south to north, and he found the MacDonalds of Skye, and MacLeod of MacLeod, as also a strong detachment of regular troops, engaged in the same service. While these forces, in number two thousand men, searched with eagerness the interior of the island, its shores were surrounded with small vessels of war, cutters, armed boats, and the like. It seemed as if the Prince's escape from a search so vigorously prosecuted was altogether impossible; but the high spirit of a noble-minded female rescued him, when probably every other means must have failed.

This person was the celebrated Flora MacDonald; she was related to the Clanranald family, and was on a visit to that chief's house at Ormaclade, in South Uist, during the emergency we speak of. Her stepfather was one of Sir Alexander MacDonald's clan, an enemy to the Prince of course, and in the immediate command of the militia of the name MacDonald, who were then in South Uist.

Notwithstanding her stepfather's hostility, Flora MacDonald readily engaged in a plan for rescuing the unfortunate Wanderer. With this purpose she procured from her stepfather a passport for herself, a man servant, and a female servant, who was termed Betty Burke—the part of Betty Burke being to be acted by the Chevalier in woman's attire. In this disguise, after being repeatedly in danger of being taken, Charles at length reached Kilbride, in the Isle of Skye; but they were still in the country of Sir Alexander MacDonald, and, devoted as that chief was to the service of the Government, the Prince was as much in danger as ever. Here the spirit and presence of mind of Miss Flora MacDonald were again displayed in behalf of the object so strangely thrown under the protection of one of her sex and age. She resolved to confide the secret to Lady Margaret MacDonald, the wife of Sir Alexander, and trust to female compassion and the secret reserve of Jacobitism which lurked in the heart of most Highland women.

The resolution to confide in Lady Margaret was particularly hardy, for Sir Alexander MacDonald, the husband of the lady to be trusted with the important secret, was, as you will recollect, originally believed to be engaged to join the Prince on his arrival, but had declined doing so, under the plea, that the stipulated support from France was not forthcoming; he was afterwards induced to levy his clan on the side of Government. His men had been at first added to Lord Loudon's army, in Inverness-shire, and now formed part of those troops from which the Chevalier had with difficulty just made his escape.

Flora MacDonald found herself under the necessity of communicating the fatal secret of her disguised attendant to the lady of a person thus situated. Lady Margaret MacDonald was much alarmed. Her husband was absent, and as the best mode for the unfortunate Prince's preservation, her house being filled with officers of the militia, she committed him to the charge of MacDonald of Kingsburgh, a man of courage and intelligence, who acted as factor or steward for her husband. Flora MacDonald accordingly conducted Charles to MacDonald of Kingsburgh's house; and he was fortunate enough to escape detection on the road, though the ungainly and awkward appearance of a man dressed in female apparel attracted suspicion on more than one occasion.

From Kingsburgh the Wanderer retired to Raasay, where he suffered great distress, that island having been plundered on account of the laird's accession to the rebellion. During this period of his wanderings he personated the servant of his guide, and the country of the Laird of MacKinnon became his temporary refuge; but notwithstanding the efforts of the chief in his favour, that portion of Skye could afford him neither a place of repose nor safety, so that he was compelled once more to take refuge on the mainland, and was by his own desire put ashore on Loch Nevis.

Here also he encountered imminent danger, and narrowly escaped being taken. There were a number of troops engaged in traversing this district, which being the country of Lochiel, Keppoch, Glengarry, and other Jacobite chiefs, was the very cradle of the rebellion. Thus the Wanderer and his guides soon found themselves included within a line of sentinels, who, crossing each other upon their posts, cut them off from proceeding into the interior of the province. After remaining two days cooped up within this hostile circle, without daring to light a fire, or to dress any provisions, they at length escaped the impending danger by creeping down a narrow and dark defile which divided the posts of two sentinels.

Proceeding in this precarious manner, his clothes reduced to tatters, often without food, fire, or shelter,

*E

the unfortunate Prince, upheld only by the hope of hearing of a French vessel on the coast, at length reached the mountains of Strathglass, and with Glenaladale, who was then in attendance upon him, was compelled to seek refuge in a cavern where seven robbers had taken up their abode—(by robbers you are not in the present case to understand thieves, but rather outlaws, who dared not show themselves on account of their accession to the rebellion)—and lived upon such sheep and cattle as fell into their hands. These men readily afforded refuge to the Wanderer, and recognising the Prince, for whom they had repeatedly ventured their lives, in the miserable suppliant before them, they vowed unalterable devotion to his cause. Among the flower of obedient and attached subjects, never did a prince receive more ready, faithful, and effectual assistance than he did from those who were foes to the world and its laws. Desirous of rendering him all the assistance in their power, the hardy freebooters undertook to procure him a change of dress, clean linen, refreshments, and intelligence. They proceeded in a manner which exhibited a mingled character of ferocity and simplicity. Two of the gang waylaid and killed the servant of an officer, who was going to Fort Augustus with his master's baggage. The portmanteau which he carried fell into the robbers' hands, and supplied the articles of dress which they wanted for the Chevalier's use. One of them, suitably disguised, ventured into Fort Augustus, and obtained valuable information concerning the movements of the troops; and desirous to fulfil his purpose in every particular, he brought back in the singleness of his heart, as a choice regale to the unhappy Prince, a pennyworth of gingerbread!

With these men Charles Edward remained for about three weeks, and it was with the utmost difficulty they would permit him to leave them. "Stay with us," said the generous robbers; "the mountains of gold which the Government have set upon your head may induce some gentleman to betray you, for he can go to a distant country and live on the price of his dishonour; but to us there exists no such temptation. We can speak no language but our own—we can live nowhere but in this country, where, were we to injure a hair of your head, the very mountains would fall down to crush us to death."

A singular instance of enthusiastic devotion happened about this time (2nd August), which served to aid the Prince's escape. A son of a goldsmith in Edinburgh, one Roderick MacKenzie, late an officer in the Prince's army, happened to be lurking in the braes of Glenmoriston. He was about the same size as the Prince, and was reckoned like him both in person and features. A party of soldiers set upon the young man in his hiding-place; he defended himself gallantly, and, anxious to render his death useful to the cause which he must no longer serve in life, he said in his mortal agony, "Ah, villains! you have slain your Prince!" His generous design succeeded. MacKenzie's head was cut off, passed for that of Charles Edward, and was sent as such up to London. It was some time ere the mistake was discovered, during which the rumour prevailed that Charles was slain; in consequence of which the search after him was very much relaxed. Owing to this favourable circumstance, Charles became anxious to see his adherents, Lochiel and Cluny MacPherson, who were understood to be lurking in Badenoch with some other fugitives; and in order to join these companions of his councils and dangers, he took leave of the faithful outlaws, retaining, however, two of them, to be his guard and guides.

After many difficulties he effected a junction with his faithful adherents, Cluny and Lochiel, though not without great risk and danger on both sides. They took up for a time their residence in a hut called the Cage, curiously constructed in a deep thicket on the side of a mountain called Benalder, under which name is included a great forest or chase, the property of Cluny. Here they lived in tolerable security, and enjoyed a rude plenty, which the Prince had not hitherto known during his wandering.

About the 18th September, Charles received intelligence that two French frigates had arrived at Lochnanuagh, to carry him and other fugitives of his party to France. . . .

The Prince landed near Morlaix, in Brittany, on the 29th September. His short but brilliant expedition had attracted the attention and admiration of Europe, from his debarkation in Boradale, about the 26th August, 1745, until the day of his landing in France, a period of thirteen months and a few days, five months of which had been engaged in the most precarious, perilous, and fatiguing series of flight, concealment, and escape that has ever been narrated in history or romance. During his wanderings, the secret of the Adventurer's concealment was entrusted to hundreds of every sex, age, and condition; but no individual was found, in a high or low situation, or robbers even who procured their food at the risk of their lives, who thought for an instant of obtaining opulence at the expense of treachery to the proscribed and miserable fugitive. Such disinterested conduct will reflect honour on the Highlands of Scotland while their mountains shall continue to exist.

COMMENTARY
WITH PARALLEL READINGS

SIR WILLIAM WALLACE

THE names of Wallace, Bruce, Douglas and Randolph never lost their magic for Scott. As a boy he had listened to tales

> Of patriot battles, won of old
> By Wallace wight and Bruce the bold.

When in *Marmion* he has to describe the disaster of Flodden he cannot help exclaiming:

> O, Douglas, for thy leading wand!
>   Fierce Randolph, for thy speed!
> O for one hour of Wallace wight,
> Or well-skill'd Bruce, to rule the fight,
> And cry "Saint Andrew and our right!"
> Another sight had seen that morn,
> From Fate's dark book a leaf been torn,
> And Flodden had been Bannockbourne!

ADVENTURES OF ROBERT BRUCE

In *The Lord of the Isles* a minstrel sings of how Bruce's brooch came into the possession of John of Lorn. Bruce, who is present in disguise with Edward his brother, objects to the minstrel's version of the tale, and gives his own.

The Brooch of Lorn

> " Whence the brooch of burning gold,
> That clasps the Chieftain's mantle-fold,
> Wrought and chased with rare device,
> Studded fair with gems of price,

On the varied tartans beaming,
As, through night's pale rainbow gleaming,
Fainter now, now seen afar,
Fitful shines the northern star?
Gem! ne'er wrought on Highland mountain,
Did, the fairy of the fountain,
Or the mermaid of the wave,
Frame thee in some coral cave?
Did in Iceland's darksome mine,
Dwarf's swart hands thy metal twine?
Or, mortal-moulded, comest thou here
From England's love, or France's fear?

" No!—thy splendours nothing tell
Foreign art or faëry spell.
Moulded thou for monarch's use,
By the overweening Bruce,
When the royal robe he tied
O'er a heart of wrath and pride;
Thence in triumph wert thou torn,
By the victor hand of Lorn!

" When the gem was won and lost,
Widely was the war-cry toss'd!
Rung aloud Bendourish fell,
Answer'd Douchart's sounding dell,
Fled the deer from wild Teyndrum,
When the homicide, o'ercome,
Hardly 'scaped with scathe and scorn,
Left the pledge with conquering Lorn!

" Vain was then the Douglas brand,
Vain the Campbell's vaunted hand,
Vain Kirkpatrick's bloody dirk,
Making sure of murder's work;
Barendown fled fast away,
Fled the fiery De la Haye,
When this brooch, triumphant borne,
Beam'd upon the breast of Lorn.

" Farthest fled its former Lord,
Left his men to brand and cord,

> Bloody brand of Highland steel,
> English gibbet, axe, and wheel.
> Let him fly from coast to coast,
> Dogg'd by Comyn's vengeful ghost,
> While his spoils, in triumph worn,
> Long shall grace victorious Lorn!"
>
> As glares the tiger on his foes,
> Hemm'd in by hunters, spears, and bows,
> And, ere he bounds upon the ring,
> Selects the object of his spring,—
> Now on the bard, now on his Lord,
> So Edward glared and grasp'd his sword;
> But stern his brother spoke, "Be still!
> What! art thou yet so wild of will,
> After high deeds and sufferings long,
> To chafe thee for a menial's song?—
> Well hast thou framed, Old Man, thy strains,
> To praise the hand that pays thy pains;
> Yet something might thy song have told
> Of Lorn's three vassals, true and bold,
> Who rent their Lord from Bruce's hold,
> As underneath his knee he lay,
> And died to save him in the fray.
> I've heard the Bruce's cloak and clasp
> Was clench'd within their dying grasp,
> What time a hundred foemen more
> Rush'd in, and back the victor bore,
> Long after Lorn had left the strife,
> Full glad to 'scape with limb and life."

The following lines from Barbour's poem, *The Bruce*, are part of the passage from which Scott took the story of Bruce and the sleuth-hound. They are given here in modern spelling, but otherwise are very little changed.

> And when he saw that he was pressed
> He quickly thought of what was best,
> And said, "My lords, we have no might
> As at this time to stand and fight;
> And therefore we must split in three,
> So all shall not assailéd be:

And in three parties hold our way."
Then to them did he also say,
In secret to the leading men,
The place where all should meet again.
And thereupon all gone are they,
And in three parties took their way.
To that place John of Lorn came then
Where the king had split his men.
Upon his track the hound he set;
It delayed not, but steady yet
Held still its course after the king,
As if it had of him knowing.
And when the king saw it pursue
His party, not the other two,
He thought they knew it was he then,
And so gave orders to his men
To split again in three, and they
Did as he said without delay,
And in three parties went on still.
The hound did then show so great skill
That it held on without changing
After the one where was the king.
And when the king has seen that they
After him all hold their way,
And follow not at all his men,
He had a great perceiving then
That they knew him; so straightway he
Did order his men speedily
To scatter, and each hold his way
All by himself, and thus did they.
Each man a different way is gone,
And the king is left alone
But for his foster-brother; so
The two together on did go.

.　　.　　.　　.　　.

The king has gone towards the wood,
Weary, worn out, in desperate mood.
Into the wood at once went he,
And held his way to a valley,
Where through the wood a water ran.
Thither in great haste went he then,

And he began to rest him there,
And said he would no further stir.
His man said, "Sir, that may not be:
Abide ye here, ye shall soon see
Five hundred yearning to kill you,
And they are many against two;
And, since we cannot deal with might,
Help us that we may with sleight."
The king then said: "Since thou wilt so,
Go forth, and I shall with thee go.
But I have oftentimes heard say
That who along a water ay
Would wade a bow-shot's length, he then
Should cause sleuth-hound and also men
To lose the scent they did pursue.
Let us see now how this will do.
For were yon devil's hound away
I care not for the rest, perfay."
Right to the stream the other men
Came, but the sleuth-hound pauséd then,
And wavered long time to and fro,
That he no certain gait could go,
Till at the last then John of Lorn
Perceived the hound the scent had lorn,
And said, "We have lost our travail;
Further to pass may nought avail;
For this wood is both broad and wide
And he is far off by this tide."

The adventures of Bruce and his foster-brother after they had escaped the hound are told, with some changes, in *The Lord of the Isles* (Canto III.st. xix.-xxxii.).

THE BLACK DOUGLAS

The grim tale of the *Douglas Larder* is told in Scott's novel *Castle Dangerous* (chapter iv.); and the fight at the church on Palm Sunday is in the same novel (chapters xix.-xx.).

The Percy and the Douglas

The following ballad is taken from Scott's *Minstrelsy of the Scottish Border*, with Scott's Introduction and Notes.

Battle of Otterbourne

The particulars of the noted Battle of Otterbourne are related by Froissart, with the highest encomium upon the valour of the combatants on each side. James, Earl of Douglas, with his brother, the Earl of Murray, in 1388 invaded Northumberland at the head of three thousand men; while the Earls of Fife and Strathern, sons to the King of Scotland, ravaged the western borders of England with a still more numerous army. Douglas penetrated as far as Newcastle, where the renowned Hotspur lay in garrison. In a skirmish before the walls, Percy's lance, with the pennon or guidon attached to it, was taken by Douglas, as most authors affirm, in a personal encounter betwixt the two heroes. The earl shook the pennon aloft, and swore he would carry it as his spoil into Scotland, and plant it upon his castle of Dalkeith. "That," answered Percy, "shalt thou never!" —Accordingly, having collected the forces of the marches, to a number equal or (according to the Scottish historians) much superior to the army of Douglas, Hotspur made a night attack upon the Scottish camp at Otterbourne, about thirty-two miles from Newcastle. An action took place, fought by moonlight with uncommon gallantry and desperation. At length Douglas, armed with an iron mace which few but he could wield, rushed into the thickest of the English battalions, followed only by his chaplain and two squires of his body.[1] Before his fol-

---

[1] Their names were Robert Hart and Simon Glendinning. The chaplain was Richard Lundie, afterwards Archdean of Aberdeen. —*Godscroft*. Hart, according to Winton, was a knight. That historian says, no one knew how Douglas fell.

lowers could come up, their brave leader was stretched
on the ground with three mortal wounds; his squires
lay dead by his side; the priest alone, armed with a
lance, was protecting his master from farther injury.
"I die like my forefathers," said the expiring hero, "in
a field of battle, and not on a bed of sickness. Conceal
my death, defend my standard,[1] and avenge my fall!
It is an old prophecy that a dead man shall gain a
field,[2] and I hope it will be accomplished this night."—
Godscroft. With these words he expired, and the fight was
renewed with double obstinacy around his body. When
morning appeared, however, victory began to incline
to the Scottish side. Ralph Percy, brother to Hotspur,
was made prisoner by the Earl Marischal, and shortly
after Harry Percy[3] himself was taken by Lord Montgomery. The number of captives, according to Wintoun,
nearly equalled that of the victors. Upon this the English
retired, and left the Scots masters of the dear-bought
honours of the field; but the Bishop of Durham approaching at the head of a body of fresh forces, not only checked
the pursuit of the victors, but made prisoners of some of
the stragglers who had urged the chase too far. The battle
was not, however, renewed, as the Bishop of Durham
did not venture to attempt the rescue of Percy. The field
was fought the 15th August, 1388.—*Fordun, Froissart,
Hollinshed, Godscroft.*

[1] The banner of Douglas, upon this memorable occasion, was
borne by his natural son, Archibald Douglas, ancestor of the
family of Cavers, hereditary sheriffs of Teviotdale, amongst
whose archives this glorious relic is still preserved. The earl,
at his onset, is said to have charged his son to defend it to the
last drop of his blood.

[2] This prophecy occurs in the ballad as an ominous dream.

[3] Hotspur, for his ransom, built the castle of Penoon, in Ayrshire, belonging to the family of Montgomery, now Earls of
Eglintoun.

BATTLE OF OTTERBOURNE

It fell about the Lammas tide,
   When the muir-men win their hay,
The doughty earl of Douglas rode
   Into England, to catch a prey.

He chose the Gordons and the Græmes,
   With them the Lindesays, light and gay;
But the Jardines wald not with him ride,
   And they rue it to this day.

And he has burn'd the dales of Tyne,
   And part of Bambroughshire:
And three good towers on Roxburgh fells,
   He left them all on fire.

And he march'd up to Newcastle,
   And rode it round about;
"O wha's the lord of this castle,
   Or wha's the lady o't?"

But up spake proud Lord Percy, then,
   And O but he spake hie!
"I am the lord of this castle,
   My wife's the lady gay."

"If thou'rt the lord of this castle,
   Sae weel it pleases me!
For, ere I cross the border fells,
   The tane of us shall die."

He took a lang spear in his hand,
   Shod with the metal free,
And for to meet the Douglas there
   He rode right furiouslie.

But O how pale his lady look'd,
   Frae aff the castle wa',
When down, before the Scottish spear,
   She saw proud Percy fa'.

"Had we twa been upon the green,
  And never an eye to see,
I wad hae had you, flesh and fell [1];
  But your sword sall gae wi' mee."

"But gae ye up to Otterbourne,
  And wait there dayis three;
And, if I come not ere three dayis end
  A fause knight ca' ye me."

"The Otterbourne's a bonnie burn;
  'Tis pleasant there to be;
But there is nought at Otterbourne
  To feed my men and me.

"The deer rins wild on hill and dale,
  The birds fly wild from tree to tree;
But there is neither bread nor kale,
  To fend [2] my men and me.

"Yet I will stay at Otterbourne,
  Where you shall welcome be;
And, if ye come not at three dayis end,
  A fause lord I'll ca' thee."

"Thither will I come," proud Percy said,
  "By the might of Our Ladye!"—
"There will I bid thee," said the Douglas,
  "My trowth I plight to thee."

They lighted high on Otterbourne,
  Upon the bent sae brown;
They lighted high on Otterbourne,
  And threw their pallions down.

And he that had a bonnie boy,
  Sent out his horse to grass;
And he that had not a bonnie boy,
  His ain servant he was.

[1] Hide. Douglas insinuates that Percy was rescued by his soldiers.
[2] Support.

But up then spake a little page,
    Before the peep of dawn—
"O waken ye, waken ye, my good lord,
    For Percy's hard at hand."

"Ye lie, ye lie, ye liar loud!
    Sae loud I hear ye lie:
For Percy had not men yestreen,
    To dight my men and me.

"But I hae dream'd a dreary dream,
    Beyond the Isle of Sky;
I saw a dead man win a fight,
    And I think that man was I."

He belted on his good braid sword,
    And to the field he ran;
But he forgot the helmet good,
    That should have kept his brain.

When Percy wi' the Douglas met,
    I wat he was fu' fain;
They swakked their swords, till sair they swat,
    And the blood ran down like rain.

But Percy with his good broad sword,
    That could so sharply wound,
Has wounded Douglas on the brow,
    Till he fell to the ground.

Then he call'd on his little foot-page,
    And said—"Run speedilie,
And fetch my ain dear sister's son,
    Sir Hugh Montgomery."

"My nephew good," the Douglas said,
    "What recks the death of ane!
Last night I dream'd a dreary dream,
    And I ken the day's thy ain.

"My wound is deep; I fain would sleep;
    Take thou the vanguard of the three,
And hide me by the braken bush,
    That grows on yonder lilye lee.

"O bury me by the braken bush,
  Beneath the blooming briar;
Let never living mortal ken,
  That ere a kindly Scot lies here."

He lifted up that noble lord,
  Wi' the saut tear in his e'e;
He hid him in the braken bush,
  That his merrie men might not see.

The moon was clear, the day drew near,
  The spears in flinders flew,
But mony a gallant Englishman,
  Ere day the Scotsmen slew.

The Gordons good, in English blood,
  They steep'd their hose and shoon;
The Lindesays flew like fire about,
  Till all the fray was done.

The Percy and Montgomery met,
  That either of other were fain;
They swapped swords, and they twa swat,
  And aye the blude ran down between.

"Yield thee, O yield thee, Percy!" he said,
  "Or else I vow I'll lay thee low!"
"Whom to shall I yield," said Earl Percy
  "Now that I see it must be so?"

"Thou shalt not yield to lord nor loun,
  Nor yet shalt thou yield to me;
But yield thee to the braken [1] bush,
  That grows upon yon lilye lee!"

"I will not yield to a braken bush,
  Nor yet will I yield to a briar;
But I would yield to Earl Douglas,
  Or Sir Hugh the Montgomery, if he were here."

[1] Fern.

As soon as he knew it was Montgomery,
  He stuck his sword's point in the gronde;
And the Montgomery was a courteous knight,
  And quickly took him by the honde.

This deed was done at Otterbourne,
  About the breaking of the day;
Earl Douglas was buried at the braken bush,
  And the Percy led captive away.

HALF-A-CROWN'S WORTH OF FIGHTING

This clan battle is described at greater length in *The Fair Maid of Perth* (chapter xxxiv). Scott there adds one very striking incident, which in reality happened at the battle of Sheriffmuir. Here is the story as Scott heard it in 1827. At Sheriffmuir the MacLeans were commanded by a chief called Hector. "In the action, as the chief rushed forward, he was frequently in situations of peril. His foster-father followed him with seven sons, whom he reserved as a body-guard, whom he threw forward into the battle as he saw his chief pressed. The signal he gave was, 'Another for Hector!' The youths replied, 'Death for Hector!' and were all successively killed."

A KING'S TRAGEDY

The story of James's murder is told in Rossetti's poem, *The King's Tragedy*.

THE LAST FIGHT OF A SCOTTISH SAILOR

The ballad which Scott refers to is given here from Percy's *Reliques*.

Sir Andrew Barton

I cannot give a better relation of the fact, which is the subject of the following ballad, than in an extract from the late Mr. Guthrie's *Peerage*; which was begun upon a very elegant plan, but never finished. Vol. i. 4to. p. 22.

"The transactions which did the greatest honour to the Earl of Surrey and his family at this time [A.D. 1511] was their behaviour in the case of Barton, a Scotch sea-officer. This gentleman's father having suffered by sea from the Portuguese, he had obtained letters of marque for his two sons to make reprisals upon the subjects of Portugal. It is extremely probable that the court of Scotland granted these letters with no very honest intention. The council board of England, at which the Earl of Surrey held the chief place, was daily pestered with complaints from the sailors and merchants, that Barton, who was called Sir Andrew Barton, under pretence of searching for Portuguese goods, interrupted the English navigation. Henry's situation at that time rendered him backward from breaking with Scotland, so that their complaints were but coldly received. The Earl of Surrey, however, could not smother his indignation, but gallantly declared at the council board, that while he had an estate that could furnish out a ship, or a son that was capable of commanding one, the narrow seas should not be infested.

"Sir Andrew Barton, who commanded the two Scotch ships, had the reputation of being one of the ablest sea officers of his time. By his depredations he had amassed great wealth, and his ships were very richly laden. Henry, notwithstanding his situation, could not refuse the generous offer made by the Earl of Surrey. Two ships were immediately fitted out, and put to sea with letters of marque, under his two sons, Sir Thomas and Sir Edward Howard. After encountering a great deal of foul weather, Sir Thomas came up with the *Lion*, which was commanded by Sir Andrew Barton in person;

and Sir Edward came up with the *Union*, Barton's
other ship (called by Hall, the *Bark of Scotland*). The
engagement which ensued was extremely obstinate on
both sides; but at last the fortune of the Howards
prevailed. Sir Andrew was killed fighting bravely, and
encouraging his men with his whistle, to hold out to
the last; and the two Scotch ships, with their crews, were
carried into the river Thames. (2nd Aug., 1511.)

"This exploit had the more merit, as the two English
commanders were in a manner volunteers in the service,
by their father's order. But it seems to have laid the
foundation of Sir Edward's fortune; for, on the 7th of
April, 1512, the king constituted him (according to
Dugdale) Admiral of England, Wales, &c.

"King James 'insisted' upon satisfaction for the death
of Barton, and capture of his ship: 'though' Henry
had generously dismissed the crews, and even agreed
that the parties accused might appear in his courts of
admiralty by their attorneys, to vindicate themselves."
This affair was in a great measure the cause of the battle
of Flodden, in which James IV. lost his life.

In the following ballad will be found perhaps some
few deviations from the truth of history: to atone for
which it has probably recorded many of the little circumstances of the story to be real, because I find one of
the most unlikely to be not very remote from the truth.
In Part ii. ver. 156, it is said, that England had before
"but two ships of war." Now the *Great Harry* had been
built only seven years before, viz. in 1503: which "was
properly speaking the first ship in the English navy.
Before this period, when the prince wanted a fleet, he
had no other expedient but hiring ships from the merchants."—*Hume*.

This ballad, which appears to have been written in

the reign of Elizabeth, has received great improvements
from the Editor's folio manuscript, wherein was an
ancient copy, which, though very incorrect, seemed in
many respects superior to the common ballad; the latter
being evidently modernised and abridged from it. The
following text is however amended and improved by
the latter (chiefly from a black-letter copy in the Pepys
Collection), as also by conjecture.

THE FIRST PART

"When Flora with her fragrant flowers
   Bedeckt the earth so trim and gaye,
And Neptune with his daintye showers
   Came to present the monthe of Maye";
King Henrye rode to take the ayre,
   Over the river of Thames past hee;
When eighty merchants of London came,
   And downe they knelt upon their knee.

"O yee are welcome, rich merchants;
   Good saylors, welcome unto mee."
They swore by the rood, they were saylors good,
   But rich merchants they cold not bee:
"To France nor Flanders dare we pass:
   Nor Bourdeaux voyage dare we fare;
And all for a rover that lyes on the seas,
   Who robbs us of our merchant ware."

King Henrye frownd, and turned him rounde,
   And swore by the Lord, that was mickle of might,
"I thought he had not beene in the world,
   Durst have wrought England such unright."
The merchants sighed, and said, alas!
   And thus they did their answer frame,
He is a proud Scott, that robbs on the seas,
   And Sir Andrewe Barton is his name.

The king lookt over his left shoulder,
   And an angrye look then looked hee:
"Have I never a lorde in all my realme,
   Will feitch yond traytor unto me?"

Yea, that dare I; Lord Howard sayes;
   Yea, that dare I with heart and hand;
If it please your grace to give me leave,
   Myselfe wil be the only man.

Thou art but yong; the kyng replyed:
   Yond Scott hath numbred manye a yeare.
"Trust me, my liege, Ile make him quail,
   Or before my prince I will never appeare."
Then bowemen and gunners thou shalt have,
   And chuse them over my realme so free;
Besides good mariners, and shipp-boyes,
   To guide the great shipp on the sea.

The first man, that Lord Howard chose,
   Was the ablest gunner in all the realm,
Thoughe he was threescore yeeres and ten;
   Good Peter Simon was his name.
Peter, sais hee, I must to the sea,
   To bring home a traytor live or dead:
Before all others I have chosen thee;
   Of a hundred gunners to be the head.

If you, my lord, have chosen mee
   Of a hundred gunners to be the head,
Then hang me up on your maine-mast tree,
   If I misse my marke one shilling bread.
My lord then chose a boweman rare,
   "Whose active hands had gained fame."
In Yorkshire was this gentleman borne,
   And William Horseley was his name.

Horseley, said he, I must with speede
   Go seeke a traytor on the sea,
And now of a hundred bowemen brave
   To be the head I have chosen thee.
If you, quoth hee, have chosen mee
   Of a hundred bowemen to be the head;
On your main-mast Ile hanged bee,
   If I miss twelvescore one penny bread.

With pikes and gunnes, and bowemen bold,
  This noble Howard is gone to the sea;
With a valyant heart and a pleasant cheare,
  Out at Thames mouth sayled he.
And days he scant had sayled three,
  Upon the " voyage," he tooke in hand,
But there he mett with a noble shipp,
  And stoutely made itt stay and stand.

Thou must tell me, Lord Howard said,
  Now who thou art, and what's thy name;
And shewe me where thy dwelling is:
  And whither bound, and whence thou came.
My name is Henry Hunt, quoth hee
  With a heavye heart, and a carefull mind;
I and my shipp doe both belong
  To the Newcastle, that stands upon Tyne.

Hast thou not heard, nowe, Henrye Hunt,
  As thou hast sayled by daye and by night,
Of a Scottish rover on the seas;
  Men call him Sir Andrew Barton, knight!
Then ever he sighed, and said alas!
  With a grieved mind, and well away!
But over-well I knowe that wight,
  I was his prisoner yesterday.

As I was sayling uppon the sea,
  A Burdeaux voyage for to fare;
To his hach-borde he clasped me,
  And robd me of all my merchant ware.
And mickle debts, God wot, I owe,
  And every man will have his owne;
And I am nowe to London bounde,
  Of our gracious king to beg a boone.

That shall not need, Lord Howard sais;
  Lett me but once that robber see,
For every penny tane thee froe
  It shall be doubled shillings three.

Nowe God forefend, the merchant said,
 That you should seek soe far amisse!
God keepe you out of that traitors hands!
 Full litle ye wott what a man hee is.

Hee is brasse within, and steele without,
 With beames on his topcastle stronge;
And eighteen pieces of ordinance
 He carries on each side along:
And he hath a pinnace deerlye dight,
 St. Andrewes crosse that is his guide;
His pinnace beareth ninescore men,
 And fifteen canons on each side.

Were ye twentye shippes, and he but one;
 I sweare by kirke, and bower, and hall;
He wold overcome them everye one,
 If once his beames they doe downe fall.
This is cold comfort, sais my lord,
 To wellcome a stranger thus to the sea:
Yet Ile bring him and his ship to shore,
 Or to Scotland he shall carrye mee.

Then a noble gunner you must have,
 And he must aim well with his ee,
And sinke his pinnace into the sea,
 Or else hee never orecome will bee:
And if you chance his shipp to borde,
 This counsel I must give withall,
Let no man to his topcastle goe
 To strive to let his beams downe fall.

And seven pieces of ordinance,
 I pray your honour lend to mee,
On each side of my shipp along,
 And I will lead you on the sea.
A glasse Ile sett, that may be seene
 Whether you sail by day or night;
And to-morrowe, I sweare, by nine of the clocke
 You shall meet with Sir Andrewe Barton knight.

THE SECOND PART

The merchant sett my lorde a glasse
  Soe well apparent in his sight,
And on the morrowe, by nine of the clocke,
  He shewed him Sir Andrewe Barton knight.
His hachebord it was "gilt" with gold,
  Soe deerlye dight it dazzled the ee:
Nowe by my faith, Lord Howarde sais,
  This is a gallant sight to see.

Take in your ancyents, standards eke,
  So close that no man may them see;
And put me forth a white willowe wand,
  As merchants use to sayle the sea.
But they stirred neither top, nor mast;
  Stoutly they past Sir Andrew by.
What English churles are yonder, he sayd,
  That can soe little curtesye?

Now by the roode, three yeares and more
  I have beene admirall over the sea;
And never an English nor Portingall
  Without my leave can passe this way.
Then called he forth his stout pinnace;
  "Fetch backe yond pedlars nowe to mee:
I sweare by the masse, yon English churles
  Shall all hang att my maine-mast tree."

With that the pinnace itt shot off,
  Full well Lord Howard might it ken;
For itt stroke down my lord's fore mast,
  And killed fourteen of his men.
Come hither, Simon, sayes my lord,
  Looke that thy word be true, thou said;
For at my maine-mast thou shalt hang,
  If thou misse thy marke one shilling bread.

Simon was old, but his heart itt was bold;
  His ordinance he laid right lowe;
He put in chaine full nine yardes long,
  With other great shott lesse, and moe;

And he lette goe his great gunnes shott:
  Soe well he settled itt with his ee,
The first sight that Sir Andrew sawe,
  He see his pinnace sunke in the sea.

And when he saw his pinnace sunke,
  Lord, how his heart with rage did swell!
"Nowe cutt my ropes, itt is time to be gon;
  Ile fetch yond pedlars backe mysell."
When my lord sawe Sir Andrewe loose,
  Within his heart he was full faine:
"Now spread your ancyents, strike up your drummes,
  Sound all your trumpetts out amaine."

Fight on, my men, Sir Andrewe sais,
  Weale howsoever this geere will sway;
Itt is my Lord Admirall of England,
  Is come to seeke mee on the sea.
Simon had a sonne, who shott right well,
  That did Sir Andrewe mickle scare;
In att his decke he gave a shott,
  Killed threescore of his men of warre.

Then Henrye Hunt with rigour hott
  Came bravely on the other side,
Soone he drove downe his fore-mast tree,
  And killed fourscore men beside.
Nowe, out alas! Sir Andrewe cryed,
  What may a man now thinke, or say?
Yonder merchant theefe, that pierceth mee,
  He was my prisoner yesterday.

Come hither to me, thou Gordon good,
  That aye wast readye att my call:
I will give thee three hundred markes,
  If thou wilt let my beames downe fall!
Lord Howard hee then calld in haste,
  "Horseley, see thou be true in stead;
For thou shalt at the maine-mast hang,
  If thou misse twelvescore one penny bread."

Then Gordon swarved the maine-mast tree,
 He swarved it with might and maine;
But Horseley with a bearing arrowe,
 Stroke the Gordon through the braine;
And he fell unto the haches again,
 And sore his deadlye wounde did bleed:
Then word went through Sir Andrews men,
 How that the Gordon hee was dead.

Come hither to mee, James Hambilton,
 Thou art my only sisters sonne,
If thou wilt let my beames downe fall
 Six hundred nobles thou hast wonne.
With that he swarved the maine-mast tree,
 He swarved it with nimble art;
But Horseley with a broad arrowe
 Pierced the Hambilton thorough the heart:

And downe he fell upon the deck,
 That with his blood did streame amane:
Then every Scott cryed, Well-away!
 Alas! a comelye youth is slaine.
All woe begone was Sir Andrew then,
 With griefe and rage his heart did swell:
"Go fetch me forth my armour of proofe,
 For I will to the topcastle mysell.

"Goe fetch me forth my armour of proofe;
 That gilded is with gold soe cleare:
God be with my brother John of Barton!
 Against the Portingalls hee it ware;
And when he had on this armour of proofe,
 He was a gallant sight to see:
Ah! nere didst thou meet with living wight,
 My deere brother, could cope with thee."

Come hither, Horseley, sayes my lord,
 And looke your shaft that itt goe right,
Shoot a good shoote in time of need,
 And for it thou shalt be made a knight.

F

Ile shoot my best, quoth Horseley then,
  Your honour shall see, with might and maine;
But if I were hanged at your maine-mast,
  I have now left but arrowes twaine.

Sir Andrew he did swarve the tree,
  With right good will he swarved then:
Upon his breast did Horseley hitt,
  But the arrow bounded back agen.
Then Horseley spyed a privye place
  With a perfect eye in a secrette part;
Under the spole of his right arme
  He smote Sir Andrew to the heart.

"Fight on, my men," Sir Andrew says,
  "A little Ime hurt, but yett not slaine;
Ile but lye downe and bleede a while,
  And then Ile rise and fight againe.
Fight on, my men," Sir Andrew says,
  "And never flinche before the foe;
And stand fast by St. Andrewes crosse
  Untill you heare my whistle blowe."

They never heard his whistle blow—
  Which made their hearts waxe sore adread:
Then Horseley sayd, Aboard, my lord,
  For well I wott Sir Andrew's dead.
They boarded then his noble shipp,
  They boarded it with might and maine;
Eighteen score Scots alive they found,
  The rest were either maimed or slaine.

Lord Howard tooke a sword in hand,
  And off he smote Sir Andrewes head,
"I must have left England many a daye,
  If thou wert alive as thou art dead."
He caused his body to be cast
  Over the hatchbord into the sea,
And about his middle three hundred crownes:
  "Wherever thou land this will bury thee."

Thus from the warres Lord Howard came,
  And backe he sayled ore the maine,
With mickle joy and triumphing
  Into Thames mouth he came againe.
Lord Howard then a letter wrote,
  And sealed it with seale and ring;
"Such a noble prize have I brought to your grace,
  As never did subject to a king:

"Sir Andrewes shipp I bring with mee;
  A braver shipp was never none:
Nowe hath your grace two shipps of warr,
  Before in England was but one."
King Henryes grace with royall cheere
  Welcomed the noble Howard home,
And where, said he, is this rover stout,
  That I myselfe may give the doome?

"The rover, he is safe, my liege,
  Full many a fadom in the sea;
If he were alive as he is dead,
  I must have left England many a day:
And your grace may thank four men i' the ship
  For the victory wee have wonne,
These are William Horseley, Henry Hunt,
  And Peter Simon, and his sonne."

To Henry Hunt, the king then sayd,
  In lieu of what was from thee tane,
A noble a day now thou shalt have,
  Sir Andrewes jewels and his chayne.
And Horseley, thou shalt be a knight,
  And lands and livings shalt have store;
Howard shall be erle Surrye hight,
  As Howards erst have beene before.

Nowe, Peter Simon, thou art old,
  I will maintaine thee and thy sonne:
And the men shall have five hundred markes
  For the good service they have done.

Then in came the queene with ladyes fair
  To see Sir Andrewe Barton knight:
They weend that hee were brought on shore,
  And thought to have seen a gallant sight.

But when they see his deadlye face,
  And eyes soe hollow in his head,
I wold give, quoth the king, a thousand markes,
  This man were alive as hee is dead:
Yett for the manfull part hee playd,
  Which fought soe well with heart and hand,
His men shall have twelvepence a day,
  Till they come to my brother kings high land.

FLODDEN FIELD

Scott's poem *Marmion* is a "Tale of Flodden Field,"
and the battle is described in Canto VI.

XIX

Even so it was. From Flodden ridge
  The Scots beheld the English host
  Leave Barmore-wood, their evening post,
    And heedful watch'd them as they cross'd
The Till by Twisel Bridge.
  High sight it is, and haughty, while
  They dive into the deep defile;
  Beneath the cavern'd cliff they fall,
  Beneath the castle's airy wall.
By rock, by oak, by hawthorn-tree,
  Troop after troop are disappearing;
  Troop after troop their banners rearing,
Upon the eastern bank you see.
Still pouring down the rocky den,
  Where flows the sullen Till,
And rising from the dim-wood glen,
Standards on standards, men on men,
  In slow succession still,
And, sweeping o'er the Gothic arch,
And pressing on, in ceaseless march,
  To gain the opposing hill.

That morn, to many a trumpet clang,
Twisel! thy rock's deep echo rang;
And many a chief of birth and rank,
Saint Helen! at thy fountain drank.
Thy hawthorn glade, which now we see
In spring-tide bloom so lavishly,
Had then from many an axe its doom,
To give the marching columns room.

XX

And why stands Scotland idly now,
Dark Flodden! on thy airy brow,
Since England gains the pass the while,
And struggles through the deep defile?
What checks the fiery soul of James?
Why sits that champion of the dames
   Inactive on his steed,
And sees, between him and his land,
Between him and Tweed's southern strand,
   His host Lord Surrey lead?
What 'vails the vain knight-errant's brand?
—O, Douglas, for thy leading wand!
   Fierce Randolph, for thy speed!
O for one hour of Wallace wight,
Or well-skill'd Bruce, to rule the fight,
And cry—"Saint Andrew and our right!"
Another sight had seen that morn,
From Fate's dark book a leaf been torn,
And Flodden had been Bannockbourne!—
The precious hour has pass'd in vain,
And England's host has gain'd the plain;
Wheeling their march, and circling still,
Around the base of Flodden hill.

XXVI

At length the freshening western blast
Aside the shroud of battle cast;
And, first, the ridge of mingled spears
Above the brightening cloud appears;
And in the smoke the pennons flew,
As in the storm the white sea-mew.

Then mark'd they, dashing broad and far,
The broken billows of the war,
And plumed crests of chieftains brave,
Floating like foam upon the wave;
　　But nought distinct they see:
Wide raged the battle on the plain;
Spears shook, and falchions flash'd amain;
Fell England's arrow-flight like rain;
Crests rose, and stoop'd, and rose again,
　　Wild and disorderly.
Amid the scene of tumult, high
They saw Lord Marmion's falcon fly:
And stainless Tunstall's banner white,
And Edmund Howard's lion bright,
Still bear them bravely in the fight:
　　Although against them come,
Of gallant Gordons many a one,
And many a stubborn Badenoch-man,
And many a rugged Border clan,
　　With Huntly, and with Home.

XXXIII

By this, though deep the evening fell,
Still rose the battle's deadly swell.
For still the Scots, around their King,
Unbroken, fought in desperate ring.
Where's now their victor vaward wing,
　　Where Huntly, and where Home?—
O, for a blast of that dread horn,
On Fontarabian echoes borne,
　　That to King Charles did come,
When Rowland brave, and Olivier,
And every paladin and peer,
　　On Roncesvalles died!
Such blast might warn them, not in vain,
To quit the plunder of the slain,
And turn the doubtful day again,
　　While yet on Flodden side,
Afar, the Royal Standard flies,
And round it toils, and bleeds, and dies,
　　Our Caledonian pride!

In vain the wish—for far away,
While spoil and havoc mark their way,
Near Sybil's Cross the plunderers stray.—
"O, Lady," cried the Monk, "away!"
   And placed her on her steed,
And led her to the chapel fair,
   Of Tilmouth upon Tweed.
There all the night they spent in prayer,
And at the dawn of morning, there
She met her kinsman, Lord Fitz-Clare.

XXXIV

But as they left the dark'ning heath,
More desperate grew the strife of death.
The English shafts in volleys hail'd,
In headlong charge their horse assail'd;
Front, flank, and rear, the squadrons sweep
To break the Scottish circle deep,
   That fought around their King.
But yet, though thick the shafts as snow,
Though charging knights like whirlwinds go,
Though bill-men ply the ghastly blow,
   Unbroken was the ring;
The stubborn spear-men still made good
Their dark impenetrable wood,
Each stepping where his comrade stood,
   The instant that he fell.
No thought was there of dastard flight;
Link'd in the serried phalanx tight,
Groom fought like noble, squire like knight,
   As fearlessly and well;
Till utter darkness closed her wing
O'er their thin host and wounded King.
Then skilful Surrey's sage commands
Led back from strife his shatter'd bands;
   And from the charge they drew,
As mountain-waves, from wasted lands,
   Sweep back to ocean blue.
Then did their loss his foemen know;
Their King, their Lords, their mightiest low,
They melted from the field as snow,

When streams are swoln and south winds blow,
   Dissolves in silent dew.
Tweed's echoes heard the ceaseless plash,
   While many a broken band,
Disorder'd, through her currents dash,
   To gain the Scottish land;
To town and tower, to down and dale,
To tell red Flodden's dismal tale,
And raise the universal wail.
Tradition, legend, tune, and song,
Shall many an age that wail prolong
Still from the sire the son shall hear
Of the stern strife, and carnage drear,
   Of Flodden's fatal field,
Where shiver'd was fair Scotland's spear,
   And broken was her shield!

THE GOODMAN OF BALLENGIECH

Other adventures of James V. in disguise are related in *The Lady of the Lake*.

THE RESCUE OF KINMONT WILLIE

This exploit is the subject of a good ballad also given in Scott's *Minstrelsy*, with his own Introduction.

In the following rude strains, our forefathers commemorated one of the last and most gallant achievements performed upon the border. The reader will find, in the subjoined extract from Spottiswoode, a minute historical account of the exploit; which is less different from that contained in the ballad than might perhaps have been expected:

Anno 1596.—"The next year began with a trouble

in the borders, which was like to have destroyed the peace betwixt the two realms, and arose upon this occasion. The Lord Scroop being the warden of the west marches of England, and the laird of Bacleuch having the charge of Liddesdale, they sent their deputies to keep a day of truce, for redress of some ordinary matters. —The place of meeting was at the Dayholme of Kershop, where a small brook divideth England from Scotland, and Liddesdale from Bawcastle. There met, as deputy for the laird of Bacleuch, Robert Scott of Hayninge; and for the Lord Scroop, a gentleman within the west wardenry, called Mr. Salkeld. These two, after truce taken and proclaimed, as the custom was, by sound of trumpet, met friendly, and, upon mutual redress of such wrongs as were then complained of, parted in good terms, each of them taking his way homewards. Meanwhile it happened, one William Armstrong, commonly called *Will of Kinmonth*, to be in company with the Scottish deputy, against whom the English had a quarrel for many wrongs he had committed, as he was indeed a notorious thief. This man, having taken his leave of the Scots deputy, and riding down the river of Liddel on the Scottish side, towards his own house, was pursued by the English, who espied him from the other side of the river, and, after a chase of three or four miles, taken prisoner, and brought back to the English deputy, who carried him away to the castle of Carlisle.

"The laird of Bacleuch complaining of the breach of truce (which was always taken from the time of meeting, unto the next day at sun-rising), wrote to Mr. Salkeld, and craved redress. He excused himself by the absence of the Lord Scroop. Whereupon Bacleuch sent to the Lord Scroop, and desired the prisoner might be set at liberty,

* F

without any bond or condition, seeing he was unlawfully taken. Scroop answered, that he could do nothing in the matter, it having so happened, without a direction from the queen and council of England, considering the man was such a malefactor.—Bacleuch, loth to inform the king of what was done, lest it might have bred some misliking betwixt the princes, dealt with Mr. Bowes, the resident ambassador of England, for the prisoner's liberty; who wrote very seriously to the Lord Scroop in that business, advising him to set the man free, and not to bring the matter to a further hearing. But no answer was returned; the matter thereupon was imparted to the king, and the queen of England solicited by letters to give direction for his liberty; yet nothing was obtained; which Bacleuch perceiving, and apprehending both the king, and himself as the king's officer, to be touched in honour, he resolved to work the prisoner's relief, by the best means he could.

"And, upon intelligence that the castle of Carlisle, wherein the prisoner was kept, was surprisable, he employed some trusty persons to take a view of the postern gates, and measure the height of the wall, which he meant to scale by ladders, and, if those failed, to break through the wall with some iron instruments, and force the gates. This done, so closely as he could, he drew together some two hundred horse, assigning the place of meeting at the tower of Morton, some ten miles from Carlisle, an hour before sun-set. With this company, passing the water of Esk, about the falling, two hours before day, he crossed Eden beneath Carlisle bridge (the water, through the rain that had fallen, being thick), and came to the Sacery, a plain under the castle. There making a little halt, at the side of a small bourn, which they call Cadage, he caused eighty of the company to light from their horses, and take the ladders, and other instruments which he had prepared, with them. He himself, accompanying them to the foot of the wall, caused the ladders to be set to it, which proving too short, he gave order to use the other instruments for opening the wall nigh the postern; and finding the business likely to succeed, retired to the rest whom he had left on horseback, for assuring those that entered upon the castle against any eruption from the town. With some little labor a breach was made for single men to enter, and they who first went in, broke open the postern for the rest. The watchmen, and some few the noise awaked, made a little restraint, but they were quickly repressed and taken captive. After which, they passed to the chamber wherein the prisoner was kept; and, having brought him forth, sounded a trumpet, which was a signal to them without that the enterprize was performed. My Lord Scroope and Mr. Salkeld were both within the house, and to them the prisoner cried, 'a good night!' The captives taken in the first encounter were brought to Bacleuch, who presently returned them to their master, and would not suffer any spoil, or booty, as they term it, to be carried away; he had straitly forbidden to break open any door, but that where the prisoner was kept, though he might have made prey of all the goods within the castle, and taken the warden himself captive; for he would have it seen, that he did intend nothing but the reparation of his majesty's honor. By this time, the prisoner was brought forth, the town had taken the alarm, the drums were beating, the bells ringing, and a beacon put on the top of the castle, to give warning to the country. Whereupon Bacleuch commanded those that entered the castle, and the prisoner, to horse; and marching again by the Sacery, made to the river at the Stony-bank, on the other side, whereof certain were assembled to stop his passage; but he causing to sound the trumpet, took the river, day being then broken, and they choosing to give him way, he retired in order through the Grahams of Esk (men at that time of great power, and his un-friends), and came back into Scottish ground two hours after sun-rising, and so homewards.

"This fell out the 13th April, 1596. The queen of England, having notice sent her of what was done, stormed not a little. One of her chief castles surprised, a prisoner taken forth of the hands of the warden, and carried away, so far within England, she esteemed a great affront. The lieger, Mr. Bowes, in a frequent convention kept at Edinburgh, the 22nd May, did, as he was charged, in a long oration, aggravate the heinousness of the fact, concluding that peace could not longer continue betwixt the two realms, unless Bacleuch were delivered in England, to be punished at the queen's pleasure. Bacleuch compearing, and charged with the fact, made answer—'That he went not into England with intention to assault any of the queen's houses, or to do wrong to any of her subjects, but only to relieve a subject of Scotland unlawfully taken, and more unlawfully detained; that, in the time of a general assurance, in a day of truce, he was taken prisoner against all order, neither did he attempt his relief till redress was refused; and that he had carried the business in such a moderate manner, as no hostility was committed, nor the least wrong offered to any within the castle; yet was he content, according to the ancient treaties observed betwixt the two realms, when as mutual injuries were alleged, to be tried by the commissioners that it should please their majesties to appoint, and submit himself to that which they should decern.'—The convention, esteeming the answer reasonable, did acquaint the ambassador therewith, and offered to send commissioners to the borders, with all diligence, to treat with such as the queen should be pleased to appoint for her part.

"But she, not satisfied with the answer, refused to appoint any commissioners; whereupon the council of England did renew the complaint in July thereafter; and the business being of new agitated, it was resolved of as before, and that the same should be remitted to the trial of commissioners: the king protesting, 'that he might, with great reason, crave the delivery of Lord Scroope, for the injury committed by his deputy, it being less favourable to take a prisoner, than relieve him that is unlawfully taken; yet, for the continuing of peace, he would forbear to do it, and omit nothing, on his part, that could be desired, either in equity, or by the laws of friendship.'—The borders in the mean time, making daily incursions one upon another, filled all their parts with trouble, the English being continually put to the worse; neither were they made quiet, till, for satisfying the queen, the laird of Bacleuch was first committed in St. Andrews, and afterwards entered in England, where he remained not long." [1]—*Spottiswoode's History of the Church of Scotland*, pp. 414, 416. Ed. 1677.

> O have ye na heard o' the fause Sakelde?
> O have ye na heard o' the keen Lord Scroop?
> How they hae ta'en bauld Kinmont Willie,
> On Hairibee to hang him up?

[1] The bishop is, in this last particular, rather inaccurate. Buccleuch was indeed delivered into England, but this was done in consequence of the judgment of commissioners of both nations, who met at Berwick this same year. And his delivery took place, less on account of the raid of Carlisle, than of a second exploit of the same nature.

Had Willie had but twenty men,
  But twenty men as stout as he,
Fause Sakelde had never the Kinmont ta'en,
  Wi' eight score in his cumpanie.

They band his legs beneath the steed,
  They tied his hands behind his back;
They guarded him, fivesome on each side,
  And they brought him ower the Liddel-rack.

They led him thro' the Liddel-rack,
  And also thro' the Carlisle sands;
They brought him to Carlisle castell,
  To be at my Lord Scroop's commands.

"My hands are tied, but my tongue is free,
  And whae will dare this deed avow?
Or answer by the border law?
  Or answer to the bauld Buccleuch?"

"Now haud thy tongue, thou rank reiver!
  There's never a Scot shall set ye free:
Before ye cross my castle yate,
  I trow ye shall take farewell o' me."

"Fear na ye that, my lord," quo' Willie:
  "By the faith o' my body, Lord Scroop," he said,
"I never yet lodged in a hostelrie,[1]
  But I paid my lawing[2] before I gaed."

Now word is gane to the bauld Keeper,
  In Branksome Ha', where that he lay,
That Lord Scroop has ta'en the Kinmont Willie,
  Between the hours of night and day.

He has ta'en the table wi' his hand,
  He garr'd the red wine spring on hie—
"Now Christ's curse on my head," he said,
  "But avenged of Lord Scroop I'll be!

[1] Inn.   [2] Reckoning.

"O is my basnet[1] a widow's curch?[2]
　　Or my lance a wand of the willow tree?
Or my arm a ladye's lilye hand,
　　That an English lord should lightly[3] me!

"And have they ta'en him, Kinmont Willie,
　　Against the truce of border tide?
And forgotten that the bauld Buccleuch
　　Is Keeper here on the Scottish side?

"And have they e'en ta'en him, Kinmont Willie,
　　Withouten either dread or fear?
And forgotten that the bauld Buccleuch
　　Can back a steed, or shake a spear?

"O were there war between the lands,
　　As well I wot that there is none,
I wuld slight Carlisle castell high,
　　Tho' it were builded of marble stone.

"I would set that castell in a low,[4]
　　And sloken it with English blood!
There's nevir a man in Cumberland,
　　Should ken where Carlisle castell stood.

"But since nae war's between the lands,
　　And there is peace, and peace should be;
I'll neither harm English lad or lass,
　　And yet the Kinmont freed shall be!"

He has call'd him forty marchmen bauld,
　　I trow they were of his ain name,
Except Sir Gilbert Elliot, call'd
　　The laird of Stobs, I mean the same.

He has call'd him forty marchmen bauld,
　　Were kinsmen to the bauld Buccleuch;
With spur on heel, and splent on spauld,[5]
　　And gleuves of green, and feathers blue.

[1] Helmet.　　　　　[2] Coif.　　　　[3] Set light by.
　　[4] Flame.　　　　　[5] Armour on shoulder.

There were five and five before them a',
   Wi' hunting horns and bugles bright;
And five and five came wi' Buccleuch,
   Like warden's men, arrayed for fight:

And five and five, like a mason gang,
   That carried the ladders lang and hie;
And five and five, like broken men;
   And so they reached the Woodhouselee.

And as we cross'd the Bateable Land,
   When to the English side we held,
The first o' men that we met wi',
   Whae sould it be but fause Sakelde?

"Where be ye gaun, ye hunters keen?"
   Quo' fause Sakelde; "come tell to me!"
"We go to hunt an English stag,
   Has trespassed on the Scots countrie."

"Where be ye gaun, ye marshal men?"
   Quo' fause Sakelde; "come tell me true!"
"We go to catch a rank reiver,
   Has broken faith wi' the bauld Buccleuch."

"Where are ye gaun, ye mason lads,
   Wi' a' your ladders, lang and hie?"
"We gang to herry a corbie's nest,
   That wons not far frae Woodhouselee."

"Where be ye gaun, ye broken men?"
   Quo' fause Sakelde; "come tell to me!"
Now Dickie of Dryhope led that band,
   And the never a word o' lear had he.

"Why trespass ye on the English side?
   Row-footed outlaws, stand!" quo' he;
The never a word had Dickie to say,
   Sae he thrust the lance through his fause bodie.

Then on we held for Carlisle toun,
    And at Staneshaw-bank the Eden we cross'd;
The water was great and meikle of spait,
    But the nevir a horse nor man we lost.

And when we reached the Staneshaw-bank,
    The wind was rising loud and hie;
And there the laird garr'd leave our steeds,
    For fear that they should stamp and nie.

And when we left the Staneshaw-bank,
    The wind began full loud to blaw,
But 'twas wind and weet, and fire and sleet,
    When we came beneath the castle wa'.

We crept on knees, and held our breath,
    Till we placed the ladders against the wa';
And sae ready was Buccleuch himsell
    To mount the first, before us a'.

He has ta'en the watchman by the throat,
    He flung him down upon the lead—
"Had there not been peace between our land,
    Upon the other side thou hadst gaed!—

"Now sound out, trumpets!" quo' Buccleuch;
    "Let's waken Lord Scroop, right merrilie!"
Then loud the warden's trumpet blew—
    "O whae dare meddle wi' me?" [1]

Then speedilie to work we gaed,
    And raised the slogan ane and a',
And cut a hole thro' a sheet of lead,
    And so we wan to the castle ha'.

They thought King James and a' his men
    Had won the house wi' bow and spear;
It was but twenty Scots and ten,
    That put a thousand in sic a stear! [2]

[1] The name of a border tune.   [2] Stir.

Wi' coulters, and wi' fore-hammers,
   We garr'd the bars bang merrilie,
Untill we cam to the inner prison,
   Where Willie o' Kinmont he did lie.

And when we cam to the lower prison,
   Where Willie o' Kinmont he did lie—
"O sleep ye, wake ye, Kinmont Willie,
   Upon the morn that thou's to die?"

"O I sleep saft,[1] and I wake aft;
   It's lang since sleeping was fleyed[2] frae me!
Gie my service back to my wife and bairns,
   And a' gude fellows that spier for me."

Then Red Rowan has hente him up,
   The starkest man in Teviotdale—
"Abide, abide now, Red Rowan,
   Till of my Lord Scroop I take farewell.

"Farewell, farewell, my gude Lord Scroope!
   My gude Lord Scroope, farewell!" he cried—
"I'll pay you for my lodging maill,[2]
   When first we meet on the border side."

Then shoulder high, with shout and cry,
   We bore him down the ladder lang;
At every stride Red Rowan made,
   I wot the Kinmont's airns played clang!

"O mony a time," quo' Kinmont Willie,
   "I have ridden horse baith wild and wood;
But a rougher beast than Red Rowan,
   I ween my legs have ne'er bestrode.

"And many a time," quo' Kinmont Willie,
   "I've pricked a horse out oure the furs;[4]
But since the day I backed a steed,
   I never wore sic cumbrous spurs!"

[1] Light.   [2] Frightened.   [2] Rent.   [4] Furrows.

We scarce had won the Staneshaw-bank,
  When a' the Carlisle bells were rung,
And a thousand men, in horse and foot,
  Cam wi' the keen Lord Scroope along.

Buccleuch has turned to Eden water,
  Even where it flowed frae bank to brim,
And he has plunged in wi' a' his band,
  And safely swam them thro' the stream.

He turned him on the other side,
  And at Lord Scroope his glove flung he—
"If ye like na my visit in merry England,
  In fair Scotland come visit me!"

All sore astonished stood Lord Scroope,
  He stood as still as rock of stane;
He scarcely dared to trew his eyes,
  When thro' the water they had gane.

"He is either himself a devil frae hell,
  Or else his mother a witch maun be;
I wad na have ridden that wan water,
  For a' the gowd in Christentie."

NOTES

On Hairibee to hang him up ?—P. 173, v. 1.
Hairibee is the place of execution at Carlisle.

And they brought him ower the Liddel-rack.—P. 174, v. 2.
The Liddel-rack is a ford on the Liddel.

And so they reached the Woodhouselee.—P. 176, v. 2.
Woodhouselee; a house on the border, belonging to Buccleuch.

The Salkeldes, or Sakeldes, were a powerful family in Cumberland, possessing, among other manors, that of Corby, before it came into the possession of the Howards, in the beginning of the seventeenth century. A strange stratagem was practised by an outlaw, called Jock Grame of the Peartree, upon Mr. Salkelde, Sheriff of Cumberland, who is probably the person alluded to in the ballad, as the fact is stated to have happened late in Elizabeth's time. The brother of this freebooter was lying in Carlisle jail for execution, when Jock of the Peartree came riding past the gate of Corby Castle. A child of the sheriff was playing before the door, to whom the outlaw gave an apple, saying, "Master, will you ride?" The boy willingly consenting, Grame took him up before him, carried him into Scotland, and would never part with him till he had his brother safe from the gallows. There is no historical ground for supposing, either that Salkelde, or any one else, lost his life in the raid of Carlisle.

In the list of border clans, 1597, Will of Kinmonth, with Kyrstie Armestrange and John Skynbank, are mentioned as leaders of a band of Armstrongs, called *Sandies Barnes*, inhabiting the Debateable Land.

JOHN BROWN, THE CHRISTIAN CARRIER

For a vivid picture of the persecuting days read Scott's novel *Old Mortality*. In chapter xlii. an incident is related very similar to the one in the text.

THE DEFENCE OF THE BASS

There is a good story about the Bass Rock—"The Tale of Tod Lapraik"—in R. L. Stevenson's *Catriona*, Chapter xv.

THE MASSACRE OF GLENCOE

Scott wrote a poem on the Massacre.

On the Massacre of Glencoe

"O tell me, Harper, wherefore flow
  Thy wayward notes of wail and woe,
  Far down the desert of Glencoe,
    Where none may list their melody?

Say, harp'st thou to the mists that fly,
Or to the dun-deer glancing by,
Or to the eagle, that from high
    Screams chorus to thy minstrelsy?"—

"No, not to these, for they have rest,—
The mist-wreath has the mountain-crest,
The stag his lair, the erne her nest,
    Abode of lone security,
But those for whom I pour the lay,
Not wild-wood deep, nor mountain grey,
Not this deep dell, that shrouds from day,
    Could screen from treach'rous cruelty.

"Their flag was furl'd, and mute their drum,
The very household dogs were dumb,
Unwont to bay at guests that come
    In guise of hospitality.
His blithest notes the piper plied,
Her gayest snood the maiden tied,
The dame her distaff flung aside.
    To tend her kindly housewifery.

"The hand that mingled in the meal,
At midnight drew the felon steel,
And gave the host's kind breast to feel
    Meed for his hospitality!
The friendly hearth which warm'd that hand
At midnight arm'd it with the brand,
That bade destruction's flames expand
    Their red and fearful blazonry.

"Then woman's shriek was heard in vain,
Nor infancy's unpitied pain,
More than the warrior's groan, could gain
    Respite from ruthless butchery!
The winter wind that whistled shrill,
The snows that night that cloaked the hill,
Though wild and pitiless, had still
    Far more than Southron clemency.

> "Long have my harp's best notes been gone,
> Few are its strings, and faint their tone,
> They can but sound in desert lone
>   Their grey-haired master's misery.
> Were each grey hair a minstrel string,
> Each chord should imprecations fling,
> Till startled Scotland loud should ring,
>   'Revenge for blood and treachery!'"

THE ESCAPE OF PRINCE CHARLES

Prince Charles appears in Scott's first novel, *Waverley*, full of charm, daring and high hopes. Another novel, *Redgauntlet*, shows him as he was a few years later with dying hopes and less gallant bearing.

If you wish to know more about Cluny Macpherson's Cage where the Prince took refuge, and to learn how David Balfour and Alan Breck were entertained there with brandy, venison, and heather-beds, and how David offended Cluny by refusing to play cards, and how Cluny won all their money and then gave it back again, you must read R. L. Stevenson's *Kidnapped*.

THE END

MADE AT THE TEMPLE PRESS LETCHWORTH IN GREAT BRITAIN

1929

KINGS TREASURIES OF LITERATURE

1s. 4d.

181. LITTLE PLAYS FROM THE GREEK MYTHS. Written and edited by Audrey Webb. 192 pp. 1s. 4d.

182. IDYLLS OF THE KING (Complete Edition). By Alfred Tennyson. 320 pp. 1s. 4d.

183. THE MARCH OF POETRY — Chaucer to Bridges. Compiled and edited by Guy N. Pocock, M.A. 256 pp. 1s. 4d.

170. TANGLEWOOD TALES. By Nathaniel Hawthorne. Edited by Guy N. Pocock, M.A. Illustrated by W. H. Birch. 256 pp. 1s. 4d.

171. A BOOK OF GIANTS AND DWARFS. Edited by G. T. Atkinson, M.A. and M. E. Atkinson. Illustrated. 256 pp. 1s. 4d.

172. **KIDNAPPED.** By R. L. Stevenson. Edited by Robert Macintyre, M.A. With a map to illustrate the wanderings by sea and land. 256 pp. 1s. 4d.

173. **TALES FROM THE ARABIAN NIGHTS.** Edited by John Garrett, B.A. Illustrated. 256 pp. 1s. 4d.

A selection of the best stories such as Sindibad of the Sea and The Magic Horse.

174. **TREASURE.** An Anthology of Treasure Quests: Worldly and Other-worldly. Compiled by Tom Staveley B.A. 256 pp. 1s. 4d.

The stories, poems and excerpts are taken from the Bible, the works of Pliny, Herodotus, Spenser, Stevenson, Masefield, Quiller-Couch, and many others. Exercises and Suggestions.

175. **MODERN SHORT STORIES.** Edited by Guy N. Pocock, M.A. 256 pp. 1s. 4d.

A collection of stories by such well-known writers as H. G. Wells, John Russell, Sheila Kaye-Smith, "Bartimæus" "Q," Joseph Conrad, and W. H. Hudson. Exercises and Suggestions.

176. **MODERN PLAYS — ONE-ACT.** Edited by A. Mordaunt Shairp, B.A. 256 pp. 1s. 4d.

The Editor who is a successful playwright as well as a schoolmaster, has made a striking and unusual collection of short plays for schools, including the works of Lord Dunsany, W. W. Jacobs, Laurence Housman, Mary Pakington, and others. With Acting Appendices.

177. DIALOGUES FROM JANE AUSTEN. Edited for schools by Joan Spearing, From the original edition by Rosina Fillipi. Illustrated. Costume Notes. 192 pp. 1s. 4d. Exercises and Suggestions.

178. THE GOOD-NATUR'D MAN. By OLIVER GOLD-SMITH. Edited by J. A. G. Bruce B.A. 192 pp. 1s. 4d.

A new school edition of Goldsmith's excellent but lesser known play, with full Commentary and Acting Appendix.

179. EXPLORATION IN AFRICA. Edited by Rev. Edwin W. Smith. With Commentaries and Maps. 256 pp. 1s. 4d.

The Editor, who has spent forty years in Africa, has selected passages from the works of the great explorers which describe the discovery of the Pygmies, The Lakes, River Sources and so forth.

180. BURNING GOLD. A Junior Poetry Book. Edited by Reed Moorhouse. 192 pp. 1s. 4d.

A delightful collection of poems suitable for younger pupils. The choice ranges from Chaucer to de la Mare, and includes works of all the great poets who have written poems loved by young people.

J. M. DENT & SONS LTD.
BEDFORD STREET, LONDON, W.C.2

~~~

VOLUMES PUBLISHED AT
1s. 0d. Each

(All volumes in light blue covers are published at 1s.)

No.

ALL OTHER VOLUMES 1s. 4d. EACH.

KINGS TREASURIES OF LITERATURE

IN NUMERICAL ORDER

*Books which include Questions and Exercises are
marked thus* *

No.		s.	d.
125. THERAS: AN ATHENIAN BOY		1	4
*126. THE RIVALS.		1	4
127. FURTHER PROSE FOR PRÉCIS		1	4
*128. CYMBELINE		1	4
*129. FOUR STORIES BY CONRAD		1	4
130. STORIES IN ENGLISH VERSE		1	4
131. FORM-ROOM PLAYS—INTERMEDIATE		1	4
*132. GREAT FIGHTS IN LITERATURE		1	4
133. THE YOUNGER CHARACTERS OF DICKENS		1	4
134. SIR WALTER RALEIGH (1552–1618)		1	4
*135. EVANGELINE AND MILES STANDISH		1	0
*136. LITTLE WOMEN		1	4
*137. BUNYIP TOLD ME		1	0
138. SOLVE SUNTRAP		1	0
139. OLD GOLD		1	0
*140. UNCLE REMUS		1	4
*141. THE ROSE AND THE RING		1	4
*142. MUCH ADO ABOUT NOTHING		1	4
143. JUNIOR MODERN ESSAYS		1	4
144. UNTOLD TALES OF THE PAST		1	0
145. FOR REPETITION		1	4
146. ENGLISH LYRICAL VERSE		1	4
*147. THE SHOEMAKER'S HOLIDAY		1	0
*148. THE WHALING STORY FROM "MOBY DICK"		1	4
*149. SHE STOOPS TO CONQUER		1	4
*150. KING LEAR		1	4
151. ALPHA OF THE PLOUGH—SERIES II.		1	4
*152. ADVENTURES AMONG BIRDS. HUDSON		1	4
*153. EOTHEN		1	4
*154. INTRODUCTION TO BYRON		1	4
*155. GULLIVER'S TRAVELS		1	4
*156. HEROES OF FICTION		1	4
157. LATER MODERN POETRY		1	4